Women Returning to
Higher Education

SRHE and Open University Press Imprint
General Editor: Heather Eggins

Women Returning to Higher Education

Gillian Pascall and
Roger Cox

The Society for Research into Higher Education
& Open University Press

Published by SRHE and
Open University Press
Celtic Court
22 Ballmoor
Buckingham
MK18 1XW

and
1900 Frost Road, Suite 101
Bristol, PA 19007, USA

First Published 1993

A catalogue record of this book is available from the British Library

ISBN 0 335 19055 3 (pb)   0 335 19056 1 (hb)

Library of Congress Cataloging-in-Publication Data
Pascall, Gillian.
    Women returning to higher education/Gillian Pascall and Roger
Cox.
        p.   cm.
    Includes bibliographical references and index.
    ISBN 0–335–19056–1   ISBN 0–335–19055–3 (pbk).
    1. Women college students – England – Midlands – Longitudinal
studies.   2. Women college students – England – Midlands – Attitudes-
-Longitudinal studies.   3. Continuing education – England – Midlands-
-Longitudinal studies.   4. Sex differences in education – England-
-Midlands – Longitudinal studies.   5. Education, Higher – Social
aspects – England – Midlands – Longitudinal studies.   I. Cox, Roger,
1946–.   II. Title.
LC2056.P37   1993
376′.65′09424 – dc20   93–13275
                                                                              CIP

Typeset by Type Study, Scarborough
Printed in Great Britain by
St Edmundsbury Press, Bury St Edmunds, Suffolk

For the forty-three women whose return to higher education shaped the content and, we hope, the spirit of this study; and for two other mature students, Mary Maxwell and Sue Parker.

Contents

Preface and acknowledgements

Research studies that involve a longitudinal element are of necessity slow in the making. Our thanks go to all those who have assisted and encouraged us over the past ten years especially the 43 women who gave their time and insights to us in the interviews. The project was begun with financial help from the Nottingham University Research Fund and completed with the help of the School of Social Studies. Particular thanks must go to our two research assistants, themselves 'women returning', to whose skilful, sensitive and knowledgeable interviewing this study owes a great deal. Sue Parker also spent many hours wrestling with the computer programme that provided us with an analysis of the second interviews and saved us much labour. Our thanks also go to Linda Poxon who transcribed all the second interviews, and to Mehtap Tatar, Fahreddin Tatar and Julia Evetts who read sections of our manuscript and made helpful and often comforting comments. Any misjudgements and misinterpretations remain our own.

All names and some details in the following text have been altered to protect identity.

List of Abbreviations

CQSW	Certificate of Qualification in Social Work
DES	Department of Education and Science
EOC	Equal Opportunities Commission
FE	further education
GCHQ	Government Communications Headquarters
HE	higher education
HND	Higher National Diploma
IRS	industrial relations services
JMB	Joint Matriculation Board
PGCE	Postgraduate Certificate of Education
RSA	Royal Society of Arts
SATs	standard assessment tasks
TOPs	Training Opportunities Programme

1

Introduction

The subject of women returning to higher education as mature students is intriguing for several reasons. One is the dramatically changing shape of women's careers, their increasing commitment to the labour market, and the way they negotiate the path between paid and unpaid work; for some women education plays a key role in their strategy to find a place in the public world after periods of childcare. Connected with this is the educational deficit of those who grew up expecting that to be an adult woman was to be a full-time housewife and who finished their first period of education in an era when opportunities in higher education were more restricted, especially for girls.

On the other hand, a significant change in educational policy is the development of policies for widening access to higher education from the traditional 18-year-old catchment. The students in this study are one of the key groups that such policies are intended to reach. They were a pioneering group for a much wider educational expansion. Because we have studied our respondents over a number of years we are able to address questions about the long-run impact of such developments, which will otherwise be invisible to those now debating and implementing them.

The study draws on transcribed interviews with 43 women at two institutions of higher education in the East Midlands in the early 1980s. Respondents were asked to reflect on their early educational experiences, careers in paid and unpaid work, decisions about returning to education, and experience of education so far. Their very eloquent accounts of the constraints of their lives, of aspirations about careers, of anxieties and excitement about change, left us with questions about what followed. We therefore built in a longitudinal element, and subsequently re-interviewed those we could trace (just over half). There are two main dimensions to these later interviews, representing public and private views of the impact of education on women's lives: firstly an account of subsequent careers, and secondly a reassessment of the educational experience in terms of personal self-fulfilment.

The work is a rich account of the way women perceive their educational experiences and draws very much on their own interpretations. It also connects with a number of theoretical traditions: work on why adults return to education, women's relationship to education systems, and the relationship between women's paid and unpaid work. In particular, this work sheds light on the way education relates to women's lives in paid and unpaid work.

This introductory chapter starts with an examination of relevant theoretical traditions concerned with the education of girls and women, with the education of adults and with education in general. There follows a review of empirical data about mature students in higher education, and an account of the approach of this study.

Women's education – reproducing domesticity?

The most important theoretical tradition for understanding the education of girls and women has been the literature about reproduction. The key claim of reproduction theories is that education systems reproduce the social relations of the wider society. For feminist writers within this paradigm these relations include the relations of reproduction as well as those of production. So, for example, in her essay 'Socio-cultural reproduction and women's education' Madeleine MacDonald aimed:

> to develop an analysis of women's education which relates the form and content of schooling to women's position in (capitalist/patriarchal) societies. The emphasis will be upon the way in which schooling produces both classed and sexed subjects, who are to take their place in a social division of labour structured by the dual, yet often contradictory, forces of class and gender relations.
>
> (MacDonald, 1980: 13)

Reproduction centres around the family and domestic life, so an important strand in this writing was to connect schools with girls' domestic futures (Deem, 1978, 1980; David, 1980). The 1980s could not produce examples of such unembarrassed promotion of domesticity as Horn uncovers in the 1890s:

> Female pupil–teachers experienced similar gender discrimination (to their pupils), since, unlike their male colleagues, they were not required to learn Euclid and algebra but had instead, by 1890, to answer a paper on domestic economy if they wished to sit for a Queen's scholarship examination for entry to a training college. And when an HMI visited their school, they had to 'afford evidence of their skill in teaching needlework, by a lesson given in his presence'.
>
> (Horn, 1988: 76)

But theorists argued that in the 1980s, domestic science still played a role in schools, and even where the overt curriculum had become more gender-neutral, there was a hidden curriculum that persuaded girls more subtly towards a future in domesticity and low-paid work:

> The provision of a form of schooling for domesticity may be one of the ways in which the conditions are ensured for the continued existence of a female reserve army of labour and an unskilled, cheap, female labour force. Such a form of schooling would also contribute indirectly to the reproduction of capitalism by encouraging a female domestic labour force, responsible for the biological reproduction and the nurturance of workers.
>
> (MacDonald, 1980: 17)

Similarly, Miriam David concluded that 'the specification of girls' domestic and maternal responsibilities and those of their teachers has been an overriding concern of the school system since its beginnings in the nineteenth century' (David, 1980: 242).

A critique of the over-deterministic character of such writing has led to accounts that describe the experience of girls within education and emphasize their ability to resist definitions offered by schools. McRobbie (1978), Griffin (1985) and Anyon (1983) offer accounts of education from the girls' point of view; these echo Paul Willis' (1977) work in their attempts to understand how and why girls accept their positions in the division of labour. These accounts start from the position that girls are more than passive recipients of messages about femininity, and they offer a rich insight into the culture of femininity within schools, the different strategies available to girls and the interaction of class and gender in the processes that lead girls to their varied destinies. For example, Anyon argues that girls and women react with 'a simultaneous process of accommodation and resistance' (Anyon, 1983: 19). Discussing educational politics she argues that:

> In conflictful situations such as these neither working-class nor more affluent females are passive; contrary to the myth, women – and girls – actively struggle to come to terms with, or to transcend, the conflicts involved in being female.
>
> (Anyon, 1983: 21)

Beginning with similar concerns, Valli (1986) gives an account of forces outside education – especially in the labour process itself and in the family – that turn girls towards a particular model of femininity. Wolpe's more recent writing is cautious about the generalization of girls' educational experiences, seeing them as more varied, and as not always totally opposite to those of boys (Wolpe, 1988).

The reproduction argument has not stood still; in her more recent publications McDonald/Arnot has shifted from the language of 'repro-duction' to the language of 'hegemony' to leave more room for negotiation:

By putting the concept of hegemony rather than 'reproduction' at the fore of an analysis of class and gender, it is less easy in doing research to forget the active nature of the learning process, the existence of dialectic relations, power struggles, and points of conflict . . . Further it allows us to remember that the power of dominant interests is never total nor secure. Cultural hegemony is still a weapon which must be continually struggled for, won, and maintained.

(Arnot, 1982: 66)

Each of these accounts gives a more guarded and complex picture of the reproduction of gender within the schools than was offered by early theories of social reproduction. Their reliance on qualitative research offers a safeguard against over-simplification as well as a lively picture of the action they seek to demonstrate. The continuing thread, though, is of reproduction. In most accounts the fundamental role of schools, work-places and families as structures that will lead girls to accept their role in domestic labour and their inferior position in paid employment is still implied. Thus the complicity of schools and families in turning girls towards a domestic life remains a taken-for-granted part of the sociology of girls' education (Acker, 1987). The girls' resistance – whether it takes the form of romance or sexuality – becomes a means by which they become ensnared in feminine destinies. Thus reproduction is moved in part to the cultural level – girls sustain the sexual division of labour too (McRobbie, 1978).

Theories of reproduction have been the subject of criticism on a wider canvas than the education literature. Their tendency to functionalism and associated lack of room for history is widely criticized. In an elegant formulation of these arguments Connell concludes that social repro-duction is:

an *object of strategy*. When it occurs, as it often does, it is an achievement by a particular alliance of social forces over others. It cannot be made a postulate or presupposition of theory. And the concept cannot take the explanatory weight that reproduction theories of gender place on it.

(Connell, 1987: 44)

Theories of reproduction make continuity central. It is entirely appro-priate to ask how gender relations are sustained, and why girls go on accepting versions of their future that disadvantage them in the division of domestic and paid labour. But it is important to ask about change too. To question whether educational structures can offer routes to change – at an individual or social level – is not necessarily to go back to a liberal idea of education as the 'golden pathway to uncountable opportunities' (Oakley, 1981: 134). Connell argues that embracing ideologies of equality is the long-term source of legitimacy by the State, and he gives 'funding women's education on a scale comparable with men's' as a direct example of a strategy that may backfire: 'Responding to challenges to the legitimacy of the political order, or even to the government of the day, involves the state in strategies that inevitably disrupt the legitimacy of domestic patriarchy' (Connell, 1987: 160).

In terms of this study, this literature poses a key question about the relationship between education for girls and women and domesticity. It is a question to which our respondents seemed to give a rather different answer than their contemporary theorists. The emphasis in the theory is on structures and their reproduction, with education forming a key element in the institutional web that keeps women ensnared. On the other hand, the accounts of the women returners were altogether more positive. They reviewed life histories in which domesticity and poor opportunities in paid work had knotted together to tie them down. They saw education as the way to untie the knot. We shall return to this key issue in our account of the study and in the conclusion.

Women's education – reproducing low-paid work?

The association of women with low-paid work is the other side of the reproduction argument. If women are destined for domesticity, with the demands of husband-care and childcare taking first place in their lives, then their place in paid work will be disadvantaged.

The evidence of empirical studies of women in paid work is indeed that women are much more likely than men to work part time, to be relatively low paid, to be segregated into 'women's work', and to be at the bottom of hierarchies (Beechey, 1987; Rees, 1992). Legislation on equal opportunities and sex discrimination has not seriously challenged these features of women's lives (Morris and Nott, 1991). In many respects our respondents fit into this well known pattern.

However, there are radical changes taking place in women's working lives, and in particular in the area of the relationship between paid and unpaid work. The length of time that women take off paid work after childbirth has been declining; concomitantly, women's attachment to the labour market has grown stronger, and their period as housewives has become much reduced. These changes have not seriously modified women's overall position in the labour market, but they have constituted a radical change in the pattern of women's careers in paid and unpaid work (Pascall, 1993). A particular feature for some of our respondents was often a gap between the expectations with which they had grown up, and their experience of extended periods in paid work.

However, the role of education in producing this pattern of paid work is not so clear. A number of our sample were relatively well qualified educationally – even before their degree studies. About half were in employment that could be described as 'careered' – even if the career inclines were not dizzyingly steep. Again, most of our respondents were looking to education to enhance their occupational opportunities, even if their views about the future were inclined to be cautious and indefinite. There are certainly accounts of low pay, of discrimination at work, and of work structures that limited horizons and opportunities. But none of our respondents points the finger at education as the problem – except in terms of educational deficit.

A period of increasing credentialism will disadvantage those who leave the labour market and seek re-entry, as compared with those whose experience is more continuous. Increasing initial opportunities for girls at school may produce better educated women, but it is perfectly possible for the initial education of girls to improve, whilst their chances of reaching the higher levels of career deteriorate, such is the accelerating force of credentialism in the late twentieth century. In such a context, the future of adult education assumes increasing significance.

On the basis of existing literature about paid work and domesticity, the impact of each on the other and the way women's lives straddle these two worlds, we gave similar space in our study to paid work and to domesticity. The assumption was that educational expectations and experience could best be understood against both backgrounds.

Decision-making

The problem of over deterministic theories is not confined to studies of gender and was, indeed, a recurring theme in the sociology of education in the 1970s especially (Karabel and Halsey, 1977; Halsey *et al.*, 1980). With the decline in interest in general theories of education, more attention over the last decade has been given to trying to explain the situation of particular groups, not least women. However, there are equal dangers in assuming that women are not subject to the social processes that those general theories tried to describe. In particular, whilst there has been a dialogue between feminist and Marxist approaches, there has been little conversation between feminists and the currently less fashionable structural-functional approaches to education. Yet it is arguable that this sociological tradition, in theory if not always in practice, did leave room for the accommodation of rational actor models of behaviour.

The use of rational, economic actor models, or utility models of behaviour might, on first inspection seem an unlikely approach to the solution of this problem, particularly in a study of women in education, but they do have the virtue of focusing attention upon individual behaviour. Hawthorne once observed that the utility model is 'axiomatic' and, hence, on its own, 'vacuous'. But, he contends, generality can be preserved and significance obtained if the values and costs (which the subjects use in their calculation of utility) are specified. In other words, utilities are evaluated in specific contexts and these can be described and specified in a way that does not detract from the appreciation of the choices that individuals actually have to make (Hawthorne, 1970: 65).

However, to this still essentially rationalist approach, Heath, in an analysis of the 'rational model of man' theory in sociology, adds the rider that, in certain contexts, what he calls 'balanced alternatives' face the decision-maker with situations where probabilities and utilities cannot be measured or even ordered (Heath, 1974). In such contexts, whatever decision is reached must be a non-rational one, and actors adopt a variety of strategies for coping with what is essentially an impossible situation; 'they may search for information or for precedents, postpone the decision, or delegate it to others or to the culture' (Heath, 1974: 201). Heath stresses one essential limitation upon any attempt to interpret evidence in terms of rational actor models. In the search for causes and for explanations of behaviour, there is always a tendency to assume that some 'rationalist' explanation exists, however latent or hidden, but as Heath points out, this is frequently not the case because in so many decision-making contexts the necessary calculations are impossible and hence no rational choice is logically available. This modification of classical rational actor models may well have particular relevance to the study of groups in society who are generally less in command of their lives, such as children or women, but the situation Heath describes should be clearly distinguished from determined behaviour which may, according to utility models, be entirely rational.

One other way of countering the over-socialized conceptions of women is to take to heart Abrams' insistence on explaining behaviour historically. In searching for explanations of individual behaviour we should seek, he argues, to see the issue 'as a problem of understanding processes of becoming rather than states of being' (Abrams, 1982: 267). Abrams applauds the sociology of deviance for establishing the importance of historical process in explaining individual behaviour, using concepts such as career to describe processes of becoming. Further, Abrams points out that the deviant career as opposed to that of a normal career is dependent upon contingencies, not randomly occurring, but having a social organization of their own:

> Where advancement in the straight career is primarily a movement through standardized, institutionally prescribed stages in a formally ordered sequence, progress in a deviant career is seen, by almost all of those who have used the concept, as a question of the negotiation of contingencies. At the same time these are career contingencies, contingent not in the sense of being merely adventitious, random occurrences but in the sense of being incident upon distinctive patterns of interaction. They are significant conjunctures of uncertain outcome, decisive moments at which the career is framed and structured one way or another.
>
> (Abrams, 1982: 271–2)

The women in this study are scarcely deviant in the more conventional sense of the term, but to some degree or other most are deviant in relation to general theories of education, as, of course, are adult students as a whole.

The emphasis upon contingencies is not unrelated to the arguments in favour of employing utility models of behaviour, in that both imply a process of negotiation with life events and with individual biographies. One further possible similarity between the deviant and the women in this study is that, at least for the period of their adolescence when important decisions affecting their futures were taken, they, like mental patients or prisoners, were subject to a degree of formal authority untypical of the constraints, however great, under which most adults live. In recognizing this, much educational research has taken this restriction to be evidence of determined and socialized behaviour; the sociology of deviance, on the other hand, has pursued the question of individual choice and of negotiation even into the mental hospital and the prison. It is precisely in contexts where the determining weight of external forces appears so overwhelming, that the methodological argument for small scale, detailed, qualitative research becomes strongest. It is only through such research that individual careers can be observed in sufficient detail to disclose what Abrams called the processes of becoming, to see social reality, 'as process rather than order, structuring rather than structure, becoming not being' (Abrams, 1982: 267). The question now arises as to whether it is possible to find an approach to explaining the process of education that can offer a general explanation and at the same time afford possibilities for understanding the particular position of women in that process.

Education theory

As already suggested, some of the more elaborate structural theories of education were produced in the 1970s, particularly when the French structuralism of Bourdieu (1977) and the somewhat functionalist American Marxism of Bowles and Gintis (1976) were confronted by the empirical tradition of mobility studies as represented by Halsey *et al.* (1980). The critical issue was the apparent inability of schooling to deliver the equality of opportunity expected as a consequence of the expansion of secondary levels of education after the Second World War. The apparent determinateness of the group, but indeterminateness of the individual within the group, had been well advertised in relation to class and education after the publication of Jencks' study, in which he pointed to the large element of 'luck' (always a metaphor for that which is not understood) in life chances, and to the apparently limited part played by education in determining an individual's future income as an adult (Jencks, 1972).

At much the same time, and partly in response to the same problem that Jencks addressed, Boudon offered an explanation of the randomness that Jencks observed. He argued that:

even if grade school education were so effective that achievement at its completion were independent of social background, the probabilities of a lower-class youngster attending college and a fortiori of attending a prestigious institution of higher education would probably remain much lower than that of an upper-class youngster.

(Boudon, 1973/4: 114)

Whilst these discussions of the 1970s focused on class and made scant reference to gender, they do have a particular significance for discussion of gender in the 1990s since what was asked about working-class boys then is being asked about girls now. Blackstone, for example, has pointed out that, in educational terms, the situation of girls is improving, but that that improvement is not reflected in advancement in the labour market (Blackstone, 1987).

Boudon is also of especial interest here because he employs a utility model of behaviour within the context of a more structural theory of mobility. In his preface Boudon poses a series of rhetorical questions relating to class that have implications also for the study of gender:

Why do lower-class people choose to get less education than higher-class people, when they know that more education would better their lot? Is not the explanation according to which people behave differently because they have different value systems a typically ad hoc or even tautological one? What of the 'radical' scheme according to which one of the latent functions of schools is to deter lower-class students from advancing too far, educationally and socially – is this not a facile view, even if it contains an element of truth . . .

(Boudon, 1973/4: xiii)

The rejection of both 'value theory', and 'school-as-the-enemy' theory is significant since both have been used to explain the educational careers of girls, though simplistic socialization theories of gender differences are now rare and there is a growing appreciation of the complexity of the relationship between schooling and gender. Whilst Boudon's tone in his preface is unduly dismissive, his approach does have some interest for us here, not least because he addresses the issue of rational choice.

Boudon attempts to distinguish between primary and secondary effects of stratification. The primary effects are those of cultural background, by which he seems to imply a determining process of socialization that restricts the intellectual abilities of those it affects; secondary effects are those not attributable to this process. Really what Boudon appears to be talking about is a two stage process that can be represented in what he calls a 'Cartesian space' whose principal dimension may be, for example, achievement at the end of primary schooling. At this, or any other, significant 'branching point' in an educational system, children of lower- and of higher-class backgrounds will be differentially distributed in what may initially be viewed as a two dimensional space. However, even if two individuals from different class backgrounds are occupying the same space at this point, add the third dimension and it will be seen that the choices they make about their future education will continue to be affected by their social backgrounds. These are the secondary effects, which mean that to aspire to a particular educational level requires a child of lower-class background to travel a greater 'social distance' than the child from a higher-class background (Boudon, 1973: 23).

Greater distance implies greater costs and the individual has to calculate benefits and costs in assessing the utility of their choice. Boudon, therefore, is suggesting a process containing two components. One relates to the determining effects of cultural background, the other to the choices individuals make given their situation. In the latter case:

> it is assumed (1) that people behave rationally in the economic sense of the concept (i.e. they attempt to maximize the utility of their decisions), but that (2) they also behave within decisional fields whose parameters are a function of their position in the stratification system.
>
> (Boudon, 1973/4: 36)

Boudon also argues that whilst the primary effects of class may be attenuated by the education process, the secondary effects increase exponentially. This has been disputed by Halsey and his colleagues for boys in England, but perhaps if their data had included evidence for girls, they might not have been so optimistic (Halsey *et al.*, 1980). Class position, and we shall argue gender position, is not a once and for all injection given at birth, but something that differentially structures the perceptions of otherwise equal educational achievers. These differences might be explained by differences in the 'value' individuals place on education, but of this explanation Boudon is highly critical. He believes it to be not even partially true, but in fact false since it can only explain why some people behave as they do, and has no capacity to explain why others in a similar situation behave differently. What does explain the variation in behaviour, claims Boudon, are the secondary effects of class, but the decisions that these entail constitute a 'rationality factor'. Since 'value theory' implies that people behave irrationally, acting against their self interest because of the values they hold, a 'value factor' and a 'rationality factor' cannot be added together to explain any variance. That being the case, the value factor cannot be an explanation, however partial (Boudon, 1973: 111). For Boudon, this objection to the mixture of values and reason as the basis for behaviour is principally on logical grounds relating to the use of variables in multivariate statistical analysis, but the point has validity in relation to the interpretation of qualitative data as well. Values, especially those attributed to a group or class of people, offer only a casual, almost lazily deterministic account of behaviour.

Applying Boudon's theory to the dimension of gender rather than class, the contrast between the primary and secondary effects of gender might be thought to be even more striking in their effects upon girls' performance in schools and beyond. Increasingly, the primary effects are negligible in terms of overall performance; if girls are initially disadvantaged by their gender (which is an increasingly problematic generalization), formal education mitigates that disadvantage to some degree as it does the disadvantage of low-class origin – girls clearly do not inhabit a different part of that Cartesian space defined by general ability. Nevertheless the 'secondary' effects of gender are well known and very striking. A girl who cannot do maths exhibits the same kind of inhibition as the working-class boy who believes all mental labour beyond him; this Boudon would presumably call a primary effect. A girl whose performance in maths matches that of the best of the boys, but who chooses to read social sciences at university may be exhibiting the secondary effects of her gender position. The distance a girl who aspires to be an engineer has to travel is very considerable; should she aspire to be a social worker, the terrain is easy and the route well sign-posted.

The importance of Boudon's approach for the study of gender lies in his insistence that though a dimension such as class or gender defines a situation for an individual and places them in a particular social position, there are still choices to be made. Whereas in the analysis of groups it may not be necessary to explore the variations within groups, for the analysis of individuals, the examination of individual motives and rationales is all important. Particularly when handling qualitative data, the relationship between individual decisions and the social position from which these decisions originate is of the greatest significance. Boudon's objection to 'value theory' is also relevant to gender. Just as class values cannot explain the variations in working-class behaviour, so gender 'values' cannot explain why some women or men hold to certain beliefs more strongly than others do.

The scenario that Boudon seems to be offering is one where that which defines the group is cultural and is determining in the sense that it presents the individual with a history (as, for example, member of the working class, or as female), which cannot be altered, but that variation within groups (that is, individual behaviour), is to be analysed in terms of utility models in which individuals negotiate the choices they make from the vantage, or disadvantage, of their own particular social position. Whilst Boudon uses the notion of social position statically to explain the continued influence of the same phenomenon, class, through its second-ary effects, it is important to recognize also that through life and particu-larly after schooling has finished, social position may itself be altered by other 'histories' joining and even displacing the original biography. For example, marriage and work may significantly change the perception of the distance that has to be travelled to reach a particular goal. For the study of mature women students a more dynamic conception of social distance is needed.

Education theory and adult students

One study of mature students that has its origins in the study of social processes rather than social groups, and, in particular, is concerned with education and social mobility, is Hopper and Osborn's study of adult students (Hopper and Osborn, 1975). It is possibly also helpful that they are reflecting in their theorizing an educational system, especially at the secondary level, that was experienced by most of the women in this study, but which has changed very considerably since then. Whilst they give only limited attention to women specifically, they do present some evidence and have some observations to make. They are also concerned with the individual's subjective experience of education, and particularly with feelings of relative deprivation (see Hopper, 1971). The theoretical starting point for the study is Hopper's thermostatic view of educational systems as engineering a process of continually 'warming up' and 'cooling out' the aspirations of the participants in order to achieve a legitimate selection of individuals for the hierarchy of economic and status positions that society requires. To work efficiently, the participants must acquire the personal and inter-personal characteristics appropriate to their future role, but whereas all societies provide some kind of status training for those who are upwardly mobile, however informally, none, according to Hopper and Osborn, provide status training for those who are downwardly mobile (Hopper and Osborn, 1975: 20). In an efficient system, there should be no adult students. As they say:

> the study of the 'social problem' of adult students and education for adults presents an opportunity to study the 'sociological problem' of how a society has organized the conduct of its selection process and some of the unanticipated consequences of its organization.
>
> (Hopper and Osborn, 1975: 13)

Adult students are of interest to Hopper and Osborn as a 'critical case' with which to test their theory. Suggesting that participation as adult students may be an 'unanticipated consequence of their previous educational experiences' – unanticipated by the system that is – they hypothesize that:

> adults who have left the labour market to return to further or higher education have done so primarily in an attempt to 'adjust instrumentally' to the difficulties they have experienced as a result of having been 'selection errors'; such adults are drawn in disproportionate numbers from those patterns of mobility and non-mobility which are defined, in part, by the educational routes characterized by initial selection followed by rejection and by initial rejection followed by selection.
>
> (Hopper and Osborn, 1975: 24)

These are students who, in effect, have had educational experiences where the system has failed to combine efficiently the experiences of warming up and cooling out, thus leaving them with feelings of 'relative deprivation', and a motivation to seek to change their situation through strategies of 'legitimate innovation'.

Hopper and Osborn found their hypothesis substantially supported amongst the groups they studied, finding evidence of higher than average levels of education (initial selection), but of subsequent downward or non-mobility (see Chapter 4). They do, however, make revisions to their thesis. Like Boudon's equally systemic view of the educational process, Hopper and Osborn use the metaphor both of system and of routes through the system. The 'critical case' of adult students, leads them to modify their view of route structures and to see them as more complex than they had previously thought. Within the school system, being in the top or bottom stream, for example, may be of as much significance as the type of school itself, as also may be the criteria upon which selection is made. Secondly, important though the educational process is in relation to social mobility, there are other routes involving informal sponsorship that may only lead back to education and to formal certification at a later date. Such informal sponsors may range from trade unions to spouses. Thirdly, the subjective interpretation of selection and rejection needs to be emphasized. Hopper and Osborn conclude:

> in categorizing individuals in terms of the labels assigned to them by the education and stratification systems the theory under-emphasizes the extent to which individuals are able to 'negotiate' their own identities, and, hence, the extent to which their own personal goals and strategies may supersede and take primacy over those which the authorities within the education system either wish or assume them to have.
>
> (Hopper and Osborn, 1975: 150)

In emphasizing 'negotiation', they reflect Abram's insistence upon the importance of career and, also, this revision of their theoretical standpoint brings them close to Boudon's view of the secondary effects as a 'rationality factor'. Interestingly, it is their discussion of women adult students that brings them to this conclusion. From the point of view of the system, they argue, the selection of females is less efficient, more prone to errors, than is the case with males. If talent is neither encouraged, nor, when it is evident, directed to appropriate goals, then there are inefficiencies in the warming up process. Consequently:

> it is . . . relatively easy to cool-out those females who are rejected subsequently, not only those whose talent was not developed and recognized, but also those who have already experienced some selective education. Traditional conceptions of gender roles provide legitimate personal justification for not continuing within the system of formal education, and, thus, rejection is experienced as suitable and not unexpected.
>
> (Hopper and Osborn, 1975: 135)

Given the 'personal and structured' obstacles that women face, Hopper and Osborn conclude that any females who do overcome these obstacles to become adult students must have been 'the most erroneous "selection errors" of all', and that they constitute a major source of potential adult students (Hopper and Osborn, 1975: 137).

In terms of their personal and interpersonal characteristics, Hopper and Osborn found a difference between female adult students aged under and over thirty (*c.* 1970). Both the younger women and the men experienced greater feelings of relative deprivation than did the older women. These feelings arose, the theory predicted, from experiences contingent upon certain patterns of mobility and non-mobility. Hence the differences between younger and older women should be related to differences in these experiences. Hopper and Osborn reach the tentative conclusion that the younger women, like the men, had experienced mobility patterns involving initial selection followed by rejection not accompanied by efficient cooling out. In addition, the older women had more successfully internalized the traditional female gender role. By contrast, the younger women said that they had feelings of role conflict and felt that their gender had militated against their staying longer in education. It is important to stress that this difference is not a consequence of age itself, but of history and the different experience of different generations of women.

Interestingly, Hopper and Osborn see the combination of mobility patterns and their relation to gender roles as being important. Whereas older women were protected against the 'pathogenic' effects of inefficient patterns of mobility because of their acceptance of the traditional gender role, younger women were exposed to feelings of relative deprivation on both counts. This is useful in directing attention not only to the obstacles that being female places in the way of success in education and the labour market, but also to the feelings of frustration and rejection that women may feel, irrespective of gender; in Hopper and Osborn's study, the younger women shared a great deal in common with men (Hopper and Osborn, 1975: 143–6).

It also demonstrates the usefulness of general theories of education in the context of expanding educational systems that suck in more and more sections of the population; the more women participate in education, the more general theories of education will become applicable to them. This is not, of course, to deny that general theories need to be modified if they are successfully to explain the experience of women as well as men. Just as Hopper and Osborn see adult or continuing education as part of the same essential process as initial education of the young, so it ought to be possible to understand those educational processes that affect both men and women (Woodley *et al.*, 1987: 7). Hopper's concepts of warming up and cooling out can be related, in terms of Boudon's theory, to changes in the perception of the social distances involved in making particular educational journeys. Boudon's somewhat static conception of the secondary effects of class, gains a dynamism from Hopper's thermostatic imagery, which, in turn, is enhanced by the added dynamic of the discussion of adult students.

What emerges from Hopper and Osborn's study is taken up by Arlene McLaren. It is, she claims, the relationship between social class, the occupational structure and gender differentiation as well as educational history that is important in explaining why adults become students (McLaren, 1981). Dealing with each of these factors in turn, McLaren observes that, although there is considerable variation in educational background, women adult students tend to be better educated than their male counterparts. As far as class origin was concerned, McLaren found that women adult students tended to come from higher social class backgrounds than men. This, of course, is the pattern for all students in higher education, but is, as McLaren points out, evidence of a class related gender division amongst adult students. As far as occupational status was concerned, however, the male adult students tended to have higher occupational status than the women. Hopper and Osborn point out that there are work-related sponsors of re-entry to education: McLaren points out that these sponsorships are likely to be more available to men than to women. The initial rejection of the men by the educational system, is compensated for by work-related sponsorship; once rejected, women who enter manual occupations have no route back to education, and hence perhaps require more in the way of cultural capital from their own backgrounds, to be able to re-enter the system (Hopper and Osborn, 1975: 143; McLaren, 1981: 252).

From the point of view of Boudon's concept of social distance, the significance of sponsorship is clearly important, since it is sponsorship (whether of people or circumstances) that is most likely to change a subject's perception of what is within the range of the possible. Whereas occupation may not be so great an incentive to women as to men, marriage may be. One of the aspects of mobility not considered by Hopper and Osborn is marriage mobility. Given the educational 'lag' between women and men until very recently together with the general rise of credentialism, the impact upon potential female adult students of mobility through marriage to a spouse with higher levels of formal education is clearly something that would repay investigation. Marriage may also provide the stable financial base for a return to the educational world, or the break up of a marriage may create the necessity to become the main earner. Other forms of sponsorship may come from the difference in outlook noted by Hopper and Osborn between their older and younger cohorts of female students. The satisfaction derived from housework and child-rearing are not to be measured independently of the culture that supports women's relation to them. As that culture is eroded, the educational system, as a selecting process, may assume more significance for women, and as Hopper and Osborn observe, the feelings of relative deprivation may increase.

The empirical evidence

There are, of course, other works about mature students, who are, as anyone who has taught them will know, an intriguing collection of people. A wealth of quantitative information is provided by Woodley (1984, 1985) and Woodley *et al.* (1987). They report a Department of Education and Sciences (DES) funded study of mature students across a wide range of institutions and courses. Between five and six thousand mature students filled in questionnaires, and some students and their teachers were interviewed. The result provides a national picture of who studies what and in which institutions. The questionnaires also attempt to dredge motivations and experiences of education. This study provides information about adult education in non-qualifying courses as well as about mature students in higher education. (It also provides a brief theoretical review.) It is supplemented by a work similar in style, though smaller in scale: Smithers and Griffin (1986) on applicants to Joint Matriculation Board (JMB) universities. This has a somewhat practical orientation, with an emphasis on access.

Smithers and Griffin questioned those who applied for but did not end up on a course of higher education, as well as those who did, and thus give some picture of the barriers to access. From the present point of view it is interesting to note their finding that the typical successful applicant for a JMB special scheme is a woman in her thirties with a grammar school background who is 'relatively well qualified in terms of O level passes and professional examinations. She is likely to have held a job with a higher social rating and to be keen to make a career'. She is also likely to be applying to study arts, economics and social studies, or education (Smithers and Griffin, 1986: 66).

Drawing mainly on this and the Woodley study, we can give an account of the demographic, educational and social features of the mature student body. The picture given of mature students across a wide range of courses is of students already relatively educationally advantaged. One-third of students in the Woodley study had qualifications above A level when they started their course; only 8 per cent of university students had been admitted with less than the standard qualification. These observations apply more strongly to women: 'women in particular appear to be channelled into courses for which they are more than adequately qualified' (Woodley *et al.*, 1987: 53).

Their conclusion about the educational background is that:

> mature students do not represent a cross-section of the population in that they are more likely to have attended selective and non-state-maintained schools, they stayed on longer at school and they emerged with better qualifications than the population as a whole. However, there are still substantial numbers who left school at an early age with no or few qualifications.
>
> (Woodley *et al.*, 1987: 57)

In terms of social class, too, the picture is skewed towards those already advantaged, again particularly for women: 'The working class was massively under-represented among mature students on both qualifying and non-qualifying courses. This bias was even more marked in the case of women' (ibid.: 71). From the perspective of this study the picture of over-representation of women in the professions appears 'somewhat anomalous'! (ibid.: 74). Our interview study helps to make sense of the uses of education by older women students who appear to be already educationally and socially advantaged.

Both Woodley *et al.* and Smithers and Griffin attempt to understand their respondents' motivations. The studies come to somewhat different conclusions about the balance between instrumental reasons and those that might broadly be called self-fulfilment. Smithers and Griffin record that self-fulfilment was mentioned by more than three-quarters of the respondents; but a close look shows that a similar proportion were looking for a new career or for an advance in an old one. Woodley *et al.* put 'instrumental' reasons high on the list for students as a whole. However, this was much less true of women: 'On the whole women were less likely to give instrumental reasons and more likely to be concerned with personal development or the subject matter itself' (Woodley *et al.*, 1987: 88). Morgan found a much more overt expression of career ambition among men; she found her women respondents reluctant to express ambition, and described their responses as 'flippant or embarrassed' (Morgan, 1981: 36). Smithers and Griffin show how the two kinds of reasons merge into one another, most obviously in the hope of finding self-fulfilment through a new career (Smithers and Griffin, 1986: 71). These studies give a hint of the complexity of motivation, but inevitably have difficulty squashing it into a questionnaire format. Weil (1989) adds a useful qualitative dimension, but with an emphasis on the learning process.

In a section on problems encountered by mature students the Woodley study finds that 'Women were much more likely to lack confidence in their abilities (49 per cent of women, as opposed to 29 per cent of men). Restrictions on study time due to family demands were felt more by women (46 per cent of men and 53 per cent of women) and those due to job demands were felt more by men (48 per cent of men versus 36 per cent of women)' (Woodley *et al.*, 1987: 121). Smithers and Griffin also found that a high proportion of married women 'suffered severe problems caused by family commitments' (Smithers and Griffin, 1986: 110). The economic stringency for men and women was differently balanced, with 'male mature students . . . much more likely than females to say that they felt worse off' (Woodley *et al.*, 1987: 127).

Students found family and friends encouraging, as did those in Morgan's study. Woodley *et al.* were not sure what to conclude:

we might conclude from this section that discouraging attitudes from significant others are so effective as a barrier to study that only those people who do not have to contend with them become mature students. Alternatively, we might conclude that the great majority of people have positive or at most neutral attitudes toward the idea of older men and women going back to study, so that discouragement is rarely met with.

(Woodley *et al.*, 1987: 141)

Morgan is positively sceptical of expressions of gratitude, peppered as they are with comments about other people's difficulties! (1981: 39). Smithers and Griffin, with a sample including those who did not proceed to a course, have some evidence of unco-operative husbands (1986).

Research findings are in accord about the success with which mature students pursue their studies. For example, Smithers and Griffin conclude that 'the mature unqualified students did at least as well as the other students in the same subjects at honours degree level, and obtained proportionally more distinctions and credits on 'other' degrees' (ibid.: 120). Woodley's title 'The older the better? A study of mature student performance in British universities' (1984) speaks for itself; his later publication adds that 'women mature students were more likely than men to graduate and, having graduated, were more likely to gain a good degree' (Woodley *et al.*, 1987: 152). Morgan too found that her sample of women students had unusually high results in the degrees with 30 out of 41 achieving upper second or first class (1981: 67).

There is an acknowledged gap in even basic information about the subsequent careers of mature students. Slowey, who was involved in the Woodley project and provides useful reviews of literature, demography, policies and practices (1987, 1988), comments that 'Probably one of the other main gaps in research on mature students in Britain is in the area of the effects which participation has on their subsequent career prospects' (Slowey, 1987). Brown and Webb have begun to fill this gap with material on Scottish students, which is mainly quantitative in style (1990, 1993), and there is similar material from Hardihill and Green (1991), Tarsh (1989) and from organizations concerned with students and graduates (Brennan and McGeever, 1987; Graham, 1991).

Morgan's study, though small, sheds useful retrospective light on the subsequent careers of its sample, all of whom qualified as teachers. Comparing their sample with a small group of men, these authors conclude that 'overall, the late return to higher education seemed to have done much more for the men than for the women' (Morgan, 1981: 45). However:

the great majority of them did in fact succeed in getting jobs quite quickly. Their anger and indignation arose particularly with reference to interviews for jobs, and, to a lesser extent, with reference to promotion.

(ibid.: 46)

Drawing in particular on Woodley *et al.* and Smithers and Griffin, we can conclude that there is a great deal of information available on mature women students in higher education regarding access, what they study, and how well they achieve, but rather little about subsequent careers. This generally high level of empirical information will be well complemented by our qualitative approach and measure of longer-term information.

The large-scale studies have not been especially concerned with gender as a key feature of women's experience of higher education, and have not therefore been especially grounded in theories about women's education or about women's lives. Morgan (1981), McLaren (1981, 1985) and Hutchinson and Hutchinson (1986) fill this gap with smaller-scale work, though the latter concern women in adult education rather than in higher. Hutchinson and Hutchinson couch their argument in terms of family change 'a completed family and most of a life to fill' (1986:7) and in terms of gender differences in educational opportunities. Women are 'victims of educational lag'(1986: 12) and suffer from 'the failure of our economic and social system to develop, extend and use the capacities of the female half of the population (1986: 19). McLaren acknowledges these elements, but emphasizes the need for career. She resists the idea that 'their "decision" is determined by their family situations' (McLaren, 1986: 88) and argues:

> Most were looking for more satisfying work, work that contributed a greater good to society, work and study that created a sense of self-satisfaction and creativity. They wanted more out of life than what the ordinary jobs usually available to women could provide.
>
> (ibid.: 89)

These studies left us with questions about the balance between family and career in the motivations and decisions of women students and in their subsequent experience.

Widening access

Our first interviews took place as policies for widening access to higher education began to gain official sanction. Our respondents took traditional routes to university and polytechnic courses, mostly through A levels. But in 1978 the DES invited some local authorities to provide access studies in order to accelerate the process and widen the base of applicants. The rapid expansion in student numbers in the early 1980s encouraged these developments. By 1984 the funding bodies had begun to offer encouragement, changing 'the climate for access and continuing education' (Wagner, 1989: 154). Political support for access was expressed in a 1987 White Paper, which declared that 'places should be available for all with the necessary qualities to benefit from higher education', and in ministerial speeches:

Women, black people and children from manual workers' homes are all under-represented in higher education. Unequal access is not just uneconomic but unfair and unjust as well.

(Robert Jackson, 1988)

When the number of 18 year olds starts to rise again in the latter part of the 1990s, the whole of higher education will be poised to expand on the basis both of this increased participation from the conventional student age group, and of new patterns of recruitment among non-conventional students.

(Kenneth Baker, 1989)

Institutional rhetoric has also changed in favour of wider access (Harrison, 1990), though this may thinly disguise a preference for standard students where they can be attracted.

Leslie Wagner concludes that 'there has been a change in the climate within which access is discussed at every level: government, funding bodies, and institutions. Access has become central not marginal; legitimate not sinful; and internal not external to higher education' (Wagner, 1989: 156). He acknowledges that funding has been less forthcoming than rhetorical change, though during the 1980s local authorities supported access developments in further education colleges and through student mainten- ance grants. These developments are debated in Fulton's *Access and Institutional Change* (1989) and these paragraphs draw from Wagner's chapter in that publication.

Our respondents entered the system in the rather cool climate of the early 1980s. Subsequent institutional change and endorsement at the political, funding body and educational levels have shown them as pioneers of this educational reform.

The present study

This study has its origins in a postal questionnaire that was sent to full-time undergraduate mature women students in two institutions of higher education in the East Midlands. It was concerned with the educational, work and domestic backgrounds of the students and with the practical problems they faced in being full-time students. From the point of view of higher education, all these students were technically 'mature', that is over the age of 21, but it was clear that for many of the younger ones the break in their education had been relatively short. In drawing up a list of those we wished to interview, therefore, it was decided only to include those who had had a substantial break of at least five years since their last full-time involvement in education. Of those approached for an interview 43 responded and the interviews with these women, together with some material taken from the original questionnaire, form the basis of Chapters 2 to 5 of this book.

The interviewing was carried out by the authors and a research assistant. In all cases, the interview was fairly structured and sought to elicit information about attitudes and feelings upon leaving school; experiences of marriage, motherhood, work and housework; the decision to return to education; and the expectations and experience of higher education itself. The questions were sometimes pointed, occasionally provocative and, where appropriate, we relayed back to the respondents comments made about similar issues in the questionnaire. With a more passive, accepting group of interviewees projecting ideas and attitudes into the discussion in this way can be a dangerous practice, but with a group who are intimately and emotionally involved with the subject of the interview and living their own lives fairly intensely, it can be a useful technique. In this case it was amply justified by the readiness with which our respondents were prepared to modify or flatly disagree with what their fellows said or with what we suggested to them.

The interviews were tape-recorded and transcribed, and the analysis is based upon these transcripts together with written comments made in the questionnaire. Even though the interview schedule was fairly tightly structured, we have only occasionally sought to quantify their responses, since post-coding would have done considerable violence to their evidence. We have, however, sought to indicate as precisely as possible the typicality of responses and, within the constraints of the space available, to offer as much as is practicable in the students' own words. Nevertheless, qualitative research is often best treated interpretively, as a process of exploration, and it is worth emphasizing the extent to which these interviews involved the respondents in making their own journeys of exploration and interpretation into their own past lives and into their present experiences.

It will be useful to provide a brief statistical summary of some of the background characteristics of the group of 43 as a whole here, though information about their educational backgrounds will be given in Chapter 2. All re-entered higher education at the end of the 1970s or the beginning of the 1980s. They were born between 1933 and 1958; 14 were in their twenties at the time of the first interview, 20 in their thirties and the remaining 9 in their forties, mostly under 45. All but two had been married, 13 for the first time in their teens and 21 for the first time between the ages of 21 and 24; 7 had first become mothers in their teens, nearly all the others in their twenties. Almost a quarter of them had, by the time of the first interview, experienced separation or divorce, and this proportion increased amongst those interviewed for a second time. We do not have information about the socio-economic background of spouses, but we do have some information about the respondents' own origins, although this should be treated with care. Of the 38 fathers whose occupation could be identified with any degree of certainty, over half were in manual jobs, just under a third in clerical jobs or self-employed, and fewer than one in eight in professional or managerial occupations. Most of the mothers seem to have had paid work for some period of their lives, fairly evenly divided between manual and clerical occupations; only four could be identified as having a professional occupation.

The degree studies of our respondents fitted the expected pattern for women mature students. There were 20 in social science, 14 in arts, 6 in education, 1 in business studies and 2 in science.

In September 1991 we began the task of tracing our 43 respondents for re-interview. Only eight were traceable from the addresses we had used in the first interview. Some had changed names (on remarriage or divorce) as well as addresses. With the help of higher education authorities, an employing education authority, and personal and professional contacts, we traced 25 women, of whom 23 were interviewed. All authorities acted with proper regard for confidentiality. The difficulties of tracing the respondents were presumably compounded by the length of time since our earlier interviews, the impact of education itself as a factor of change in respondents' lives, the relatively low visibility of women in sources such as telephone directories; and the customs of changing names on marriage and divorce and of following partners' careers. The success of this exercise owed everything to the ingenuity and determination of Sue Parker, who acted as temporary research assistant for this purpose. The results may be presumed to be biased in favour of the more stable, in terms of relationships and careers (though there are no ways in which the re-interviewed group stand out from the rest demographically or educationally).

The second interviews took the same form as the first: a semi-structured interview schedule, using quotations from the earlier interviews as prompts, taped and transcribed. They were shared between one of the authors and Sue Parker, who also coded the results into Qualpro for rather more efficient analysis than was possible at the time of the first interviews. Chapters 6 and 7 draw mainly on this material.

2

Leaving School

Thoughts about school

The women in this study belong to those generations of children who went to secondary school between the end of the Second World War and the coming of the comprehensive school; almost all took the 11 plus examination and predominantly their secondary school experience was of girls' grammar schools. It was also a period when boys achieved more examination passes than did girls, both at O level and especially at A level, and women made up only a third of the undergraduate population (see Hopper and Osborn, 1975: 134). At each branching point of the system the secondary effects of gender were significant in reducing the numbers of girls who went on to the next stage.

Asked what school had meant to them in the year or so before leaving, most of these mature students expressed themselves somewhat neutrally. A few were unreservedly hostile, describing it as 'imprisonment' (Moira) or as an 'absolute bore' (Claire), and themselves as 'very alienated' (Kath). Equally a few were unreservedly enthusiastic. Marilyn expressed pride in the status of her grammar school and its uniform and Paula simply found the whole thing 'fantastic, absolutely marvellous'. On the whole, however, both hostility and rapture were muted; the emotions recollected after an intervening period of up to twenty years filled with marriages, careers and motherhood had left a rather sober impression: for Marjorie it was a question of 'get on, do the work, take the exams and get out' and for Michelle the final thought was 'thank God it's all over'. More than one remarked that by the time they left they felt they had simply had enough, that a period of drift had come to an end and, unlike the departure from primary school, leaving warranted no tears.

However, as Table 1 shows, they had had relatively successful school careers and, in this, they were similar to the broader spectrum of adult students discussed in other studies (Hopper and Osborn, 1975; Woodley et al., 1987, Morgan, 1981). Particularly striking was the fact that all but

Table 1   Highest school leaving qualification by type of school

	Selective[1]	Non-selective	Total
No qualifications	4	4	8
O levels	19	4	23
A levels	12	0	12
Total	35	8	43

Note: [1] Includes one student who took A levels at a comprehensive school.

eight of the 43 had been to selective secondary schools, and fewer than one in five had left with no formal qualifications. But this does not tell the whole story, since in several cases the practice of streaming at secondary school had been significant. Positively it provided the spur, particularly in secondary modern schools. Marilyn described herself as a 'tearaway' but that was, she thought, because she was in the A stream which was the 'be all and end all' of her life. However, being put into a lower stream was clearly a damaging experience. As Rhona put it, 'once I'd been labelled as B stream, I stopped working and just wasn't bothered'. Marjorie also recalled the importance of streaming in her selective school, where 'the A stream went to university, the B stream training colleges, the C stream – right, well you're a girl – get a clerical job'. Joy also recalled the significance of gender in an attitude that said that non-top-stream secondary modern girls could 'have any old job' until they got married, and Eleanor remembered her headmistress saying, 'well, in actual fact, you'll all leave and have babies'. There was, however, little general feeling that school had misjudged or mistreated them; the cause of their leaving at 15 or 16, or of failing to go on to higher education was attributed, in the main, to their own lack of judgement, or to circumstance.

In a small minority of cases, life events shattered or seriously disturbed family stability whilst the respondents were still at school: death of the principal earner causing major financial problems, long illness, mental breakdown, parent's divorce and remarriage, being told to leave home by parents – all these contingencies of life affected some of the women in this study. Again there were examples of these disasters reasserting gender roles. For example, May, at a private school, lost her father, and whereas her older brother continued at school and went on to university, she left school at 15. Higher education was not really considered for her, she said, not only because she was a girl, but also because of an erratic school performance and because her brother was older. For Val her mother's illness and death took her from the 'express' stream of a grammar school to the post of unpaid housekeeper, banishing further thoughts of education. Her father informed the school by letter of her impending departure, without consulting her at all; ironically the mother had had the greater earning power.

The event of marriage itself, or even the presence of a potential partner had a dramatic effect upon future educational careers in several instances. Felicity left school, 'because I knew I was going to get married, you see'. Alison, who was already engaged at school, decided against higher education because her fiancée threatened to leave her if she went away to college. Barbara actually had a university place, but having met her future husband, simply did not wish to go away, and went out to work instead. She detected a division between those heading for university or teacher training college who were interested in careers and those who were 'quite into getting married'.

Lesley became pregnant after leaving school and had to relinquish a place at teacher training college, but further education had not really been part of her life's plan in any case. She recalled being very ill-prepared for her interview and performing, she felt, badly. Even though she was offered a place, she said, 'it was just like water off a duck's back, sort of thing, I was just swept along with what was happening at the time.'

Boy friends could have a more insidious effect as Paula related: 'When I was 15, I met my husband and from being top of the class and thinking that school was absolutely everything, I then went down to the middle of the class.' She left school after taking O levels and at the age of 17 eloped to Gretna Green. For Deirdre, it was the other way round. At a grammar school, she was heading for university along with many of her peers, who, though they felt marriage was important in their lives, intended to wait until they had finished their courses. However, she failed to obtain the necessary A level grades to gain entrance to university. Instead, she became engaged to the man she was 'courting' at the time: 'I went on a secretarial course and was married a year later, which I think was quite significant really. I wouldn't have been able to do that if I'd gone to university, which would have been a good thing.' Her mother, however, was obviously pleased: 'She said I was getting too studious, and she does believe that women should be married and having children.' The marriage lasted six years.

Thoughts about work and marriage

For the women in this study the anticipation, even in the abstract, of marriage and motherhood complicated the planning of education and career. However, it was equally clear that, apart from those who married very soon after they left school, work was uppermost in their minds at this time; indeed it was seen as a necessity for all those who were not going on to further or higher education:

Well, I'd got to earn money – you must earn your living so I had to.

(Eleanor)

I took it for granted that I would [work] because I had to get the things I wanted.

(Moira)

I thought that I would work . . . for money, not really anything other than that, so that I can get on, earn money to get on.

(Paula)

Just somewhere to go and get money, really – so I could go out and have a good time.

(Rae)

Most rejected the idea that, as adolescents, they viewed work as just a stopgap between work and marriage. As Felicity remarked, 'I didn't think of it as a stopgap between marriage and children. It was just something you had to do when you left school, like you had to do your O levels before you left.' Moira insisted, 'I never imagined that I would get married or have children.' The reasons for working had to do with economic independence, albeit of a limited kind, and with the need to consume.

In terms of Boudon's thesis, leaving school is a major branching point, however. For some, the social journey the fulfilment of their dreams would have entailed was just too great. Belinda, who wanted to be a barrister, realized that 'it was almost impossible for somebody in the social position in which I was and for a woman'. Thirty years later she finally embarked upon a law degree. Susan dreamed of staying at school and of becoming a teacher, but this involved higher education: 'I saw it as a kind of "out of reach thing" – I saw it as a way to be a teacher, which I saw as being the peak of ambition – it was like an impossible dream, all right for other people.' Her parents had turned down for her a place at grammar school. Years later her ambition was realized and she was able to teach, but even after graduation that did not come without a struggle.

Quite a few did have careers in mind, in teaching, nursing or the Civil Service. Such jobs are the classic occupations for well-educated women and the reasoning for this, as adumbrated by May's private girls' school, was still remembered by her: 'It was considered quite important that you had a job which involved some kind of service.' More frequently remarked upon was the distinction between office and factory work, and here the sense of attainable mobility was clear. If teaching was not a possibility, then Susan wanted to work in an office, for her 'that was the ideal – you could go dressed up'. Similarly Marjorie, from the C stream of her grammar school, felt that 'to actually work in an office was all that was seen as the aims really of myself and my parents'. Martha, very conscious of her working-class background, claimed that apart from the few 'who had nice accents . . . everyone else assumed they would get a job, and if it wasn't a factory . . . then it was a step up, as far as their parents were concerned.' One or two recalled tussles over the kind of career that was appropriate and sensible. In particular Cathy had her heart set on going to art school, but she remembered: 'various people tried to persuade me to become a hair-dresser, or window-dresser and what have you'. However, her opposition had been firm. 'No way. I saw myself as an artist right from the start.' Even within a gender-defined world there were still battles to be fought.

There were one or two, however, who even at the relatively young age of leaving school were relating their careers to possible future marriages and families. Isabel recalled that all her friends 'had the same idea about a sort of career and then marriage in their twenties'. Dorcas, with a steady boyfriend whilst still at school, said that she did think in terms of a career, 'but relative to marriage. One that would fit in with marriage and children.' She qualified as a teacher just before she married.

In a similar situation, Lindsay explained her situation like this:

> It's difficult to look back and think what you were like so many years ago but, no, I don't really think I was very career minded, I mean, you know, as I say I'd met my husband by then and I think my thoughts were more to things that fitted round our life together rather than me as a career person. Although I did decide what I wanted to go into, you know, we hadn't planned to marry particularly early, but I did want to go into employment where I would continue education alongside working, which is what I did.

She left school with A levels, worked as a clerical officer in local government, completed a Diploma in Municipal Administration, and was married at 19. In her attempts to recapture the state of her mind some 13 to 15 years previously, Lindsay illustrated well the mixture of determinacy of background and indeterminacy of the future. A happy, conventional family background led her to anticipate marriage and a family of her own, supported by her convent grammar school, no doubt. As she said: 'You looked around and people were married and that was what you expected of life.' On the other hand, parents were opposed to early marriage and, steady boyfriend not withstanding, she saw marriage only 'at some distance in the future'. In this context work was not at the time seen as a stopgap, whatever the later judgement may have been, but as something that took place for some women at a time of indeterminacy. Marriage may be expected, but the contingent nature of the need to meet the right partner means that unlike careers it cannot be planned for in any sensible use of that term. Asked if she expected to work for a substantial part of her life, Lindsay captured perfectly the ambiguity of the meaning of work for many women: 'I don't know that I was really that well planned at the time, I suppose I just probably – I won't say drifted because I didn't – but on the other hand I don't think I'd very definite plans for what my life was going to be like.'

This rejection of the idea of work as a stopgap between school and marriage, and yet at the same time an acknowledgement of the contingent nature of that period of transition from school to adult life, is important because it illustrates well the way in which gender can be introduced into

Boudon's metaphor of social distance with its implications for looking toward future events. For these women the difficulty was not merely that the secondary effects of gender reasserted themselves, though clearly this did affect their visions of the future, but also the fact that marriage itself was an uncertain event.

Schooling in the second half of the twentieth century is increasingly about certification for the purpose of obtaining employment, and that fact (though some may have rebelled against it) was the experience of the majority whose qualifications placed them far above the average for their respective generations. They had, in Hopper and Osborn's terms, been 'warmed up' and there was a clear sense that school career affected job prospects, and particularly the prospect of keeping out of the factory. Work itself was essential, if not initially for economic reasons in the sense of material survival, then certainly for the purpose of becoming a consumer in the short term and possibly because waged labour might become a permanent necessity. Marriage, on the other hand, massively though it was supported by family history and cultural expectations, was only an abstraction, a generalized expectation unless it became a concrete possibility in the shape of a suitable partner. When this happened, as we have seen, there were frequently dramatic consequences for both schooling and work.

The secondary effects of gender, therefore, reasserting themselves at the critical branching of life at the end of schooling, produced a kind of suspended animation, which they negotiated in a variety of ways. Some consumed, having a good time, and waited for tomorrow; others set their sights on women's careers in nursing, teaching or administration – and waited for tomorrow. For some, the waiting was clearly an unhappy period of their lives. Heather, for example, at grammar school but with no scholastic background in either parents or elder siblings, scraped a couple of O levels and left, having spent her final year 'dossing around' and disliking prefects who were 'snobby or creepy'. Like several others she was determined to avoid production line work: 'because I knew it would drive me nuts', but her 'very small' ambitions produced no clear career ambitions. This was partly due to lack of confidence:

> A couple of my friends worked in the Trustees Bank and I thought they must have been much more cleverer than me because they got . . .
> I hadn't even got the confidence to go along for an interview. I was totally without confidence.

But lack of qualifications was also a problem. A sudden desire to enter social work had led to a visit to the careers office only to find that further qualifications would be necessary. 'So,' she said, 'I just ended up doing one crummy job after another until I got married.' For her, waiting was a restless, frustrating process. Her first clerical job, she found 'really interesting till I got the hang of it, then I was bored to tears, but I never seemed to know where I was going from there.' This combined with the break-up of her parents' marriage, which deeply upset her, seemed to destroy any sense of identity or purpose: 'I don't think I started thinking of myself until I got married and had the children. I just drifted from one thing to another.' The sense of waiting ended only with marriage at the age of 19 and the subsequent birth of her children, about whose mothering she was unashamedly enthusiastic. Her response to being asked if work was regarded as a stopgap between school and marriage was full of the sense of suspended animation, and the recollection was painful: 'Possibly, having talked about it since, I probably did. I think it was probably just like you say, a stopgap between school and marriage and that was it. God, it's awful when you look back, isn't it?' The sense of relative deprivation in Heather was strong, though, like most of our other respondents, she blamed no one for her school failures.

Nevertheless, it was clearly an error that had to be corrected and that provided the motivation to begin (when she felt her children were old enough to be left to their father), by assaulting that *bête noire* of so many girls of her generation – Maths O level. From 12 per cent in her 'mock' at school to a pass at evening class was a great event; as she said, 'nothing's ever meant as much as passing that one'. Almost 25 years after leaving school, Heather did find a career as a special needs teacher, working in a school that clearly set high professional standards, which she admired, but which she seemed to find a little threatening. In a job that she clearly enjoyed, and in which she was very much involved, she nevertheless resisted career ambitions and seemed to need the relative safety of the all-female group of special needs teachers, doing a teaching job that is often seen as characteristically 'female'. There remained still a shadow of that lack of confidence that had bedeviled her on leaving school. The social distance that she travelled, and which we shall discuss in relation to other respondents in Chapter 7, was considerable, but even so the secondary effects of gender lingered, constraining her visions of the possible.

The influence of parents

Schooling

When asking our respondents to reconstruct earlier parts of their lives, we asked directly about the educational and occupational backgrounds of their parents and of their siblings. Some two-thirds of the parents of these women had received their education in non-selective schools, which in effect meant that they had left school without any formal qualifications. Given that most parents had received their education sometime between 1920 and 1950, this is not surprising and not untypical (Halsey *et al.*, 1980).

But one fact does stand out as of potential significance. At least six identified a father or mother who had been offered a place at a selective school, but had not taken it up for financial reasons:

My mum, you wouldn't believe, won a scholarship to a grammar school in Scotland, but her parents couldn't afford to send her. The uniform and different reasons. Went into a sweet factory.

(Martha)

My father was quite able academically. . .but unfortunately he was the youngest of a large family, and he was offered a place at grammar school, but they couldn't afford the uniform and so he never got there. But he was always an able man and always a very interested man.

(Belinda)

My mother got a scholarship to the Girls' High School, but she didn't go because her parent's weren't well enough off. Obviously this would have meant staying at school, and the quicker she got out to work the better, she felt.

(Marilyn)

Other disruptions to parents' education were also mentioned, one of the more obvious being the Second World War and its aftermath:

He's very good at technical drawing and he wanted to be an architect. He went to the School of Building in London and started his training as an architect, and he was called up then for National Service so that put paid to that. And then he took over his own father's business so he never went back then.

(Lindsay)

He went to grammar school, but the war came so he didn't go to university.

(Rhona)

In fact, Rhona's father gained a BEd degree as an adult, making Rhona a second-generation mature student. Claire and Val both had fathers who had had to leave school for family reasons. Similarly Deirdre described her father as 'very frustrated in his ambitions really because he left school . . . in the middle of the higher certificate course, in order to take his mother away from home'.

What these recollections suggested was not only a lack of educational opportunity for their parents, but also perhaps a sense that it was felt as a loss; that, in Hopper and Osborn's terms, relative deprivation was a feature of the experience of the parent's generation too. Lindsay, for example, said, 'my mother is a very clever woman actually, but she never really had the opportunities for the education that I think she could have done justice to.'

There were, of course, some parents who had neither themselves received, nor wished for their children any more education than was absolutely necessary. Susan, for example, whose parents were both cotton mill workers, found they were not encouraging about school. They 'saw everyone's role to go to work, earn some money and be self-supporting', and 'they just didn't understand the educational system at all'. Similarly Eleanor was told on reaching the school leaving age, 'now you must earn some money', and Jenny seemed to have experienced the same incomprehension regarding the possible benefits of more education:

> I've never had any encouragement from my family to carry on with education at all, even though I did have a record of doing rather well. But I think that was to do with their background. They didn't really know anything about it.

Miriam longed to stay at school, but family problems prevented it:

> I can remember talking to friends in that year about who was leaving to take jobs, who was deciding to stay on, and minding, in a way, that some of those that were leaving along with me wanted to leave so much, because I wanted to stay on and wasn't being allowed to.

Miriam's mother, who had had a boarding school education and professional training as a nurse, was ill in hospital after the death of Miriam's sister; her father, one of those unable to take up his place at grammar school, 'didn't really understand in the same way about education'.

Marilyn, when asked if she had thought of staying longer at school commented that 'if anyone had asked me, I might, but in my life it wasn't even considered'. The fact that her mother was one of those who had had the chance of secondary schooling but not been able to take it, seemed not, in this instance, to have left the sense of lost opportunities that was evident elsewhere.

For one or two, gender was clearly an issue. Yvonne, for example, got little support from her mother whom she described as illiterate, and from her father only the conviction that, 'Girls are going to get married and education is wasted. Education is for boys because they're bread-winners.' Her brother went to university. Jean, too, found a similar attitude coming from her mother, to the effect that 'it's not worth educating a girl because she gets married and has children'. One or two other parents, appeared to have adopted a fairly *laisser-faire* attitude. Moira, for example, whose father had been to grammar school but remained a miner like his father, herself went to grammar school but found her parents unsupportive. 'They neither interfered with me in any way to encourage me at school, nor did they discourage me. They left it entirely up to me. I felt I could have done better with a bit more encouragement.' Other parents were clearly taken aback by their daughters' success. But whereas Isabel had parents who 'were rather pleased and surprised that we'd turned out as we did', Joanne only found disbelief: 'I don't think they thought I was capable.' Summoned to school by the headmaster to discuss the possibility of Joanne staying on they found that 'they couldn't cope with it, that their daughter should be fit to go on'. There was then evidence of a lack of support and sponsorship by parents, and it was not entirely from parents who, themselves, had received only the minimum education.

The weight of evidence suggested a generally supportive and positive attitude by parents to their daughters' education. Rae's parents had both left school at 14 yet nevertheless both placed great importance on her education and were disappointed with her O level failures. Barbara was brought up by an aunt who ran a hotel and was described as 'very unacademic indeed', but she was never hostile to education and encouraged her charge to go on to higher education. Glenys called her mother an 'education fanatic' who was prepared to go out to work to pay for private education, but it was not a fanaticism that could be translated into specific help or advice, because 'they didn't channel my education at all . . . we never discussed it at home'.

One or two parents led by example: Rhona's father, for instance, whose BEd we have already noted, or Cathy's mother who was 'a great self-educator', leaving school at 14, but educating herself for a career as a private secretary and still attending evening classes at the age of 73. Meryl's mother had been educated at a direct grant school, married an engine driver and initially worked as a secretary. Later, however, she returned to higher education to train as a teacher.

Another interesting group were those parents of first-generation grammar school children who were frankly admiring of their children's achievements. Felicity's mother, who had gone into service at the age of 11, was 'very proud' that her daughter went to grammar school and 'told everybody', though it appeared that she still assumed her daughter would leave school as soon as possible. Heather's parents found the situation quite straightforward. 'It was a case, I got to grammar school so I must be clever. My brother and sister went to secondary schools . . . they weren't clever and that was that.' Isabel probably reflected the feelings of her slightly bemused parents when she said, 'I was very pleased to have got to the grammar school because it was totally competitive at that time, and from the background that I came from, it was thought to be a great achievement . . . I suppose I realized that education opened doors, and gave advantages compared with my parents' life.'

Parents, however, could be embarrassingly enthusiastic. Paula's mother may have missed the chance of a grammar school place herself because her widowed mother could not afford to send her, but she was clearly ambitious for her daughter and remained so when Paula set out on the road back to higher education:

> Mum's a little bit that she brags me off . . . 'Our Paula's doing this, our Paula's doing that. She is doing ever so well.' I would keep saying, 'Mum, I'm not doing any better than anyone else. There is lots of people doing this.' She would say, 'Shut up, I know what I'm saying. You'll get through.' And they never think how I can fail as well.

In some cases the support had come from only one parent, and that the one with more education. Janet's father had been to grammar school and whereas her mother seemed uninterested, he 'was interested in a lot of things and tried to involve us in them'. Kath was aware of a difference in the educational and class background of her parents, her mother having been to a selective school; there was also educational success on her mother's side of the family in the shape of a brother with a PhD. We shall look again at her educational and career history in Chapter 7. More actively felt, if not specified, was the pressure from Deirdre's father, himself frustrated by the interruption to his own education and 40 years of being a clerk. Both parents were initially involved. 'They never visibly pushed me, but I think there was a lot of pushing in the sense they wanted me to achieve what they hadn't.' But her mother's ambition was clearly of a limited kind and she never wanted her daughter to go on with her education; indeed, as we have seen, she feared Deirdre's studiousness and welcomed her early marriage. For Sarah, it was the other way round; her mother was 'quite a driving force really', but her father could not see why education was so important for a girl.

Staying on after the compulsory school leaving age was a new opportunity for most of the families in this study in the sense that the history of the parents provided few precedents. Ignorance about the workings of secondary education was widespread, and knowledge of opportunities beyond school very limited indeed. In such a situation, whatever the opportunities, there was no presumption that they would be pursued, and Boudon's secondary effects exerted their influence, acting as a barrier to and restraint upon further educational progress. Class and educational history are the two major factors at work here, rather than gender, which, though it is by no means absent, appears as secondary to a process of social and economic change reflected in a process of educational expansion. To the extent to which they were caught up in these processes, the families of these women shared a very typical, discontinuous experience from one generation to the next. Parents, with little to assist them in their own histories, were unable to present their offspring with clear pictures of what the next educational steps might bring. Some simply opposed, by reference to their own experience; more supported, but perhaps without the skill that experience might have provided, and very few could offer their own careers in higher education as models.

What the women in this study recalled in their parents was perhaps most significantly the sense of relative deprivation; if so it may well have been, in many obscure ways, passed on in an intensified way to their daughters, to be worked out eventually in their struggles to become mature students and to challenge those secondary effects of class, educational history and gender that inhibited them when they left school. Val's family history illustrates the combination of circumstance, history and uncertainty that could all too easily generate such feelings. Her mother had been trained as a teacher and was, in fact the principal wage-earner until her death during Val's teenage years. As the only girl among three brothers, her father assumed she would take on the responsibilities of housewife. The mother's death destroyed the educational careers of all the children it would seem, since the boys too were forced into jobs. Val's school was merely informed, without her knowledge, that she was leaving. Up to that point her educational career had been highly successful, and she had been in the fast stream of her grammar school where she had taken O levels at the age of 15. With his wife's death, Val's father seemed to have been completely disorientated, but the origins of this lie deeper than the immediate family trauma. Of working-class origin, he had some educational aspirations but these were thwarted by the need to earn money. With a wife in a professional occupation he achieved some measure of affluence; there were always lots of books in the house, and his daughter described him as intelligent, and very strict and puritanical in his attitude to work and play. But the pieces of the jigsaw did not fit together in a way that allowed him to explain, or perhaps understand, the relationships between education and mobility, culture and affluence:

> As far as I can tell he was only ever interested in outcomes. He has no idea of the hard work involved or maybe that you should work at something that you are interested in. He sees little cash registers everywhere; that's always been his attitude as long as I can remember. He likes the status and the things that go with high earning power, and high prestige, but he doesn't seem to have any idea of what is involved in actually getting there. And he never gave us any . . . he never told us why we should do our homework or why we shouldn't go out at night, or why we shouldn't do this or that. It was always . . . he was very, very authoritarian, very strict. He came from a puritanical Scottish back- ground and when he spoke you just did as you were told.

Here is a sense of relative deprivation, born of a frustrated early glimpse of educational opportunity, nurtured by an achievement of affluence that was felt, possibly, to be almost illegitimate since it involved dependency; suddenly the affluence was cruelly threatened and the dependency exposed. This sense of deprivation was then visited upon the children and, perhaps, upon the daughter in particular, engendering feelings of anger and of guilt:

> The one thing that I had to take into account was my own nature. I used to wish that I was the sort of person who could stop at home and be content with that. But I wasn't. I was one of the sort of people who was disobedient. I would nip out of the back window, nip off to the pub, come back at two in the morning and never get caught. I used to think I was a very bad, wicked sort of person, no moral fibre, and that my father was right obviously. And I had two younger brothers, and my place should have been at home looking after them. I just resented it. I wished I hadn't been so Christian. It would have been much easier. I fought back.

Her parents' educational opportunities and possibilities for status mobility, as well as illness and death, made up the material influences upon her childhood, just as divorce rates, gender-related divisions of labour and, again, educational opportunities were to influence her adult life.

Work

The status of work for women is undoubtedly problematic, but this should not lead to the conclusion that parents have no interest in, or concern about, the kind of jobs their daughters do, nor indeed about careers for them in a more general sense. There were some parents as well as children for whom money was a primary consideration. Marilyn, in the top stream of a secondary modern and aware of its educational privileges in terms of learning shorthand and typing, nevertheless had as a priority to 'get a job – bring in money for the house'. Her brother, too, left grammar school at 15 and went to work because their father had died. Isabel was possibly responding to the fact that her parents 'were rather hard up', when seeking a career as a librarian through work, rather than through more education. Eleanor had to battle against parental indifference to training; her father especially 'thought it was a real bore that I kept on about it', and Yvonne rebelled against the logic of her father's attitude, which she said would have taken her into a factory or a shop.

On the whole, though, there was parental interest and concern about work. Some, like Alison's parents, offered general enthusiasm and admiration to a daughter with three A levels to her credit: 'They just said, you can do anything you want to do, and you are capable of it, so do it.' Others had to be more direct. 'The big threat when I was young was that, if you didn't work in school, you'll have to work in Woolworths' (Rhona). One or two parents were disappointed. 'I was a disappointment to my parents in terms of not getting five O levels that were required for the levels of the jobs that I wanted' (Michelle); 'My father was very keen that I should do a teacher training course, but I think he realized it was wishful thinking' (Lindsay). Parental concern was expressed in terms of the usual criteria. Jenny's parents, for example, whilst showing little interest in education were 'very concerned that I got a job that was a decent job', and Marjorie's parents shared her own aspirations for a clerical rather than a manual job. Sometimes the classic conflicts arose as with Joan whose love for horses was not, she recognized, going down too well with her parents as the basis for a career. She seemed, however, to have steered clear of open conflict:

> I wanted to work with horses but, after doing O levels, I couldn't see my parents really agreeing to me pursuing a career with horses. It caused great trouble actually. Not with my parents: with me. It was the trouble I anticipated it would cause.

Sometimes parents were concerned but their daughter was not. Felicity was asked if the kind of job she got mattered to her:

To me? I always had my mother pushing me: 'You don't want any old job the same as you don't want any old lad.' To me? No, I don't suppose so. Only in so far as mother could swank to the neighbours about it, if I got a decent job. That's all.

In different ways there seems to have been a desire by many parents to establish their daughters in work as a safeguard against the contingencies of life. 'I was going to go into the Civil Service, which was what my parents wanted me to do, you know, a nice secure job' (Sally). Kath, too, seemed to have sensed that her father, if not her mother, was anxious for her to establish some kind of independence in the form of a career against the uncertainty of marriage, whilst Dorcas's mother had to deal with a more imminent threat of marriage. Teacher training, was completed – just – before her daughter married the man she had met whilst still at school, but aspirations towards medicine had to be abandoned. In Dorcas's case there was sufficient presumption of the value of professional training for a compromise to be achieved, but in Paula's case there was a clear conflict over career images. Her mother was pushing, perhaps unrealistically, for her daughter to be a vet, but Paula, 'got this picture of somebody about 45, fat, no men friends, tweed suits, black shoes', hated taking examinations in any case, and decided that Gretna Green was the only possible solution.

Influence of siblings

Living lives that run along close parallel lines, always within sight of each other, siblings have somewhat curious relationships. There are influences, of course, but they are of a less obvious kind than those of parents or teachers who exert a direct authority, and different again from those of the peer group, which exerts its own especially intense if transitory pressure. Crudely, those women who had brothers and sisters could be divided into two groups. A smaller group of about seven or eight could be described as academically isolated in their educational achievements, in that they had attended a selective school, nearly always a grammar school, whilst their siblings had been at non-selective schools. In three cases, those of Alison, Joan and Lesley, this isolation was quite marked in that they had taken A levels at school, whereas neither siblings, nor indeed parents, appeared to have had any formal qualifications. There were several others who were the sole family representatives at grammar school, and this isolation did provoke some comment:

He's [brother] totally different. Hasn't done O level or anything. Stayed on at school until about 18 (*sic*) and just couldn't get them. Just wasn't the same as me at all.

(Alison)

They [two sisters] went to technical college, and I think they did a couple of O levels each, but I was the one who went to grammar school

. . . it was just circumstances militated against them, so they didn't
realize their full potential.

(Vera)

I was the only one to pass the 11 plus, so in that sense I was a bit of an
outcast at home, because nobody had gone to grammar school.

(Claire)

Whilst the grammar school was a major sponsor of social mobility during
the first two-thirds of the twentieth century, it clearly had its limits,
especially for girls. Without the support of precedents amongst either
parents or siblings, the chances of evading the secondary effects of class
when leaving school, of seeing possibilities of which there was no family
experience, of narrowing the social distance to be crossed were indeed very
slim. Perhaps as many as a quarter of these women would fall into the
category of those whose families offered no precedents for higher
education of any kind. A much larger group did have precedents, however,
not so much in their parents but in their siblings. As many as 15 or more
could be identified as having a brother or sister, or both who had achieved,
either at school or in their early career, a status that was discernibly higher
than that of their sisters represented in this study. This is a very mixed
group but with some interesting features to it.

One or two failed to obtain or were denied places at selective schools.
Susan, for example, had two older sisters at grammar school, but since the
second sister had been very unhappy there it had been assumed that she too
would not like it. In spite of obtaining a place, therefore, she did not go,
though she did manage to take some O levels at her secondary modern
school. Joy was unfortunately the only one of her family not to obtain a
place at grammar school. She was naturally upset. 'It was dreadful –
absolutely heartbreaking.' Gwen also had a sister at grammar school when
she was at a secondary modern, and several who themselves went to
grammar schools, had sisters who outstripped them in some way. Seven
sisters trained as teachers, together with a nurse and a social worker, all
achieving professional qualifications of relatively higher status than their
sisters in this study.

There was also a strong suggestion that gender played a significant part
here. Some three-quarters of the brothers whose schooling could be
identified were at selective schools as against considerably less than
two-thirds of their sisters. There was a group of about a dozen whose
brothers appeared to have achieved higher status in terms of education or
occupation. In a few cases, there was a clear difference in the attitude to the
education of brothers and sisters. Penelope, for example, had a much
younger step-brother who was sent to public school. Circumstances had
clearly changed, but, as she said, 'there was much more emphasis on his
education'. She it was, too, who had observed that in her mixed grammar
school the aspirations of the girls were not as high as those of the boys. The
reputation of the school rested, it seemed upon the achievements of the

boys. May had a brother who stayed at school and went on to university, in spite of the financial difficulties that seemed to have been a contributory factor in her leaving, and Yvonne's brother also went to university, though her father clearly discouraged her from any such intention. Marilyn, who with her sister went to a secondary modern, had a younger brother at grammar school. Geraldine had older brothers at the same school as herself and her younger sister, and this caused problems for the girls. 'We all went to the same school, and we had to follow in the previous one's footsteps. The boys were put as paragons of virtue, almost, and we all had to live up to that.'

When sisters were more successful at school than brothers, there was sometimes a need to re-establish the brother's reputation. Miriam and her elder sister went to grammar school, for example, whilst her brother had to be content with a comprehensive school, but this was not as it should have been, according to her: 'I really think my brother should have been at grammar school because he has passed a lot of his examinations in the Navy.' Amongst the brothers there is also evidence of more extended post-school education and of professional qualifications. Dorcas's brother went to university and became a solicitor, an occupation also taken up by Deirdre's brother; Paula's gained Higher National Diploma (HND) qualifications and became an environmental health officer; Martha's went to a Polytechnic and became an accountant, an occupation shared by the brothers of Penelope and of Geraldine.

A few had both brothers and sisters who outstripped them. Joy, coming to terms with her secondary modern, had a sister who trained as a teacher, and a brother who gained engineering qualifications. Miriam not only had a successful brother in the Navy, but also a sister who was a teacher; Lindsay had another sister at university and a brother with post-graduate qualifications in mathematics.

Lesley presented an unusual but interesting case. She had been the sole family representative at grammar school, had done quite well and was propelled by her school towards teacher training, without, as she acknowledged, really knowing what was happening to her. Pregnancy prevented her taking up her place and she spent several years drifting around jobs, getting married and bringing up two children. Her brothers and sisters, on the other hand, without being in any way spectacular, seemed to have made more solid progress in their lives; her sister especially, perhaps, working for herself and offering a book-keeping and accountancy service. Whilst the education system can sponsor, or warm up in Hopper's terminology, it can sometimes do so too quickly for the individual to readjust to the vistas that it opens up: work on the other hand sometimes allows the individual to move at their own pace and to assess the situation and its possibilities in their own terms without having to place heavy reliance upon the advice of others. This seemed to have been the situation for Lesley: 'Going through the grammar school system, you see, you were. I think, made to believe that you were superior. And this was my conflict, because although I was from a working class background, I couldn't see myself working in a factory.' Of her brothers and sisters, she said: 'None of them passed their 11 plus. They're in pretty well-paid jobs – have made their own way. So I sometimes look back and think, "Well, was it wasted, what I did?" They seem to be quite happy with their lives.'

This, then, was the background from which our mature students came. They were the heirs of the 1944 Education Act, and in many ways the beneficiaries of it, but they were often the first generation of their family to catch a glimpse of education beyond school. Whilst sponsorship from school or home was often in evidence, it was not sufficient to pull them into the stream of those whose natural destiny was higher education. They shared an experience of that complex relationship between class and the relatively tightly structured education system of post-war Britain, but to that experience must be added that of gender which was clearly of the greatest significance. These two forces appeared to have operated in somewhat different ways. At this stage, gender was not perceived as problematic (though it was to become more so); it was a determining factor of a largely negative kind in so far as the academic education most of them received did not engage directly with the issue except to say that, if they were failing academically, they could always go and have babies. Gender acted rather as a constraint upon the vision of the future: marriage was a pre-occupying possibility, but an uncertain event. Later in their lives, gender became something to negotiate self-consciously, whereas at school it was only the consequences of an assigned gender that had to be coped with. Class, on the other hand appeared to be a source of uncertainty; education offered the possibility of mobility but (beyond the desire to keep out of the factory) of a rather unfocused kind. There was more conscious-ness of class origins and class futures as problematic, and certainly in retrospect, the feelings of relative deprivation, of a failure to match educational potential to success in the adult world were quite strong. As we shall see in the next chapters, for these women gender became more problematic, more a focus for discontent and ambition, but it is important to remember that their class and educational origins were also potential sources for a sense of relative deprivation, and provided the underlying basis for the motivation to return to higher education.

3

Careers: Public and Private

Educational background may best illuminate why women turn to education as mature students, rather than to other sources of change. This section asks why they should want to change at all. It looks at women's accounts of their lives after leaving school, in terms of paid employment and the family. Our questions allowed women to talk about their experiences as paid worker, wife, housewife and mother and the way these roles interacted. The context in which the decision to return to education was taken will be examined here. The next chapter looks more closely at the decisions themselves.

For two reasons it is especially interesting to look at the way women experience interactions between paid employment and traditional domestic roles. One is the recent rapid increase in women's employment – which indicates more women combining paid work with traditional roles in the family. The other is the increasing emphasis in theoretical and empirical research on the interaction between women's paid and unpaid labour. Beechey has long argued that women's paid work can only be understood in terms of their unpaid household labour. Summarizing earlier work, she writes: 'I argued that the reasons why women constituted a distinctive kind of labour force did not lie in "natural" differences of strength and skill, as Marx had suggested, but in the sexual division of labour within the home.' She favoured 'an approach which links the spheres of production and reproduction and analyses the way in which gender is constructed in both' (Beechey, 1987: 9–11). Walby argues for a one-way relationship – that women's acceptance of unpaid work can only be understood in terms of the discriminatory terms under which they enter the labour market (Walby, 1986). Both make the relationship between paid and unpaid work central, whichever way it is understood.

Empirical studies have begun to capture the complex and changing pattern of women's working lives. Thus Martin and Roberts (1984) provide a large-scale statistical study of women's employment with essential data about the experience of different age cohorts of women workers, patterns of combining paid and unpaid work, and the resulting occupational mobility. They show that women's working lives are often characterized by disjunctions rather than by continuity. Few women follow the traditional men's pattern of 40 pensionable years in an occupation. Women are crucially affected by domestic responsibilities, and often switch between paid and unpaid work. The losses imposed on women by such switches are documented by Joshi (1987, 1991). Brannen and Moss (1991) combine empirical and theoretical insight in their study of 250 households where women combined full-time employment with motherhood.

Discrimination in the labour market and the domestic division of labour form a series of snares for girls leaving school and become the key constraints within which women go on to organize their lives. We saw both paid employment and domestic roles as important in providing a context for decisions about returning to higher education. We found that women most often described the interaction between them as critical to their need for change and their decision to make that change through a new educational career.

Our interviews allow us to look at questions about the shape of women's working lives, and the way in which paid and unpaid work affected each other. The interviews are particularly well attuned to asking about how women dealt with the constraints that each form of work imposed, what strategies they employed, and about the satisfactions and frustrations they experienced. It should be noted that these women were to some degree self-selected for frustration. Choosing higher education itself indicated their perception of a need for change.

The popular division of women into career women and housewives is much too crude a classification to describe these respondents. Most women described a much more complex history. Most had been 'housewives' in some sense, but they had also been full- and/or part-time paid workers, students, voluntary workers, and sometimes several of these at once. The two who had not married at the time of the first interview were 'career women' by default rather than clear intention, and their situation could well have changed. Some of the more 'career minded' women in the sample gave indications of turning down opportunities on account of family responsibilities.

Their lives and the decisions about turning to higher education can be best understood in the context of both paid and unpaid work. Careers are plainly affected by unpaid work and responsibilities – especially responsibilities towards children. But decisions about being a housewife are also affected by job prospects. There were a few who had suffered a blow in one area of life – being made redundant or a child leaving to live with the other parent were two examples – and whose decisions stemmed directly from a single crisis. But for more it was the way the two worlds interacted that gave rise to their chief frustrations and the decisions to make changes.

Women here are characterized as much by the pattern of their working lives as by their particular job label: career followed by children, children followed by career, career on soft pedal while the children are young, career without children, period of being a full-time housewife or not. There were very clear distinctions between those who had had a career and those who had done more mundane work, but SRNs and clerical workers could find themselves similarly ill-placed in the job market when they had responsibilities for young children.

Public careers – paid work

Jobs and careers

Escape from the dolls' house provides the most powerful image for describing women turning to higher education. And in a way this study was designed to find this. We interviewed only women old enough to have had time to leave the education system, marry, and have children. All but two had indeed married, and three-quarters had children. But all of those interviewed had some experience of paid employment, almost all full time. Again, almost all were looking to a future in which paid work loomed large. Paid work was the aspect of their lives most obviously amenable to change through educational qualifications, and it figured prominently in accounts of their return to education.

But experiences of paid work were disparate, and 'human capital' varied. There were women passionately involved in careers to which they could not go back, and women in routine jobs to which they would not return. The sample contained career nurses who had done up to 19 years in nursing, women who had skipped from one clerical job to another in a desperate fight against boredom, and women whose lives were a patchwork of different occupations, often full-time work followed by babies and a complex of part-time jobs, childcare and A levels.

For these reasons, and because of the inadequacy of the customary tools in relation to women's employment, occupational classification was not straightforward. Here we describe our respondents in terms of a main full-time occupation, and in terms of a career path. The first does some violence to the variety of many respondents' working lives, and the second meets difficulties in the fine shading of promotion and career decline (see Brannen and Moss, 1991: 55–7 for a discussion of these problems).

The relatively high educational qualifications of the sample were reflected in their work experience. A high proportion had full-time careers in the professions (17) or Civil Service (4). Most of the professional employees were in teaching, nursing or radiography, with representatives from nursery nursing, residential social work and librarianship. They were thus in traditional women's careers, with less than full professional status in most cases. Nevertheless these women had careers rather than jobs.

Another 22 were in office work: banking, secretarial and clerical jobs (16) or other white-collar jobs such as tracing or telegraphy (6). Some of these might appear to have had scope for promotion; indeed men in apparently similar positions might have had career prospects, but in practice the women found their paths blocked.

Factory work, cleaning and sales figure in these women's accounts of their work experience, but only as secondary, part-time jobs to which they resorted when their job path was broken by children.

We also attempted to identify aspects of career. To what extent were women in careers rather than jobs? Was there any degree of upward movement in their work histories? What was the shape of their working lives so far? In examining career paths we counted any element of career promotion as upward mobility. Similarly we counted any element of reduction in status as downward mobility (for example, nurses who lost status on becoming part time). We counted mobility within and between occupations.

About half of the sample (21) had achieved some promotion or long term development. It should be remembered that fairly small improvements are measured here. Many of these were in professions such as nursing, but this number includes some white-collar workers.

Nineteen were defined as static: they may have changed jobs but they remained at the same general level, and in career terms they seemed wholly blocked. These include the occasional teacher whose general level appeared unchanged, but most were secretarial, bank or other white-collar workers.

Thirteen were identified as losing status after a career break (10 of these being previously upwardly mobile). Respondents were not specifically asked to identify loss of status, and the number may therefore be higher than this. This pattern of reduced job status after career breaks is documented in Martin and Roberts (1984) and elaborated by Brannen and Moss who record that: 'Discontinuity of employment has major negative consequences for occupational mobility' (Brannen and Moss, 1991: 55). In their sample, 'nearly two-thirds of the downwardly mobile worked on a temporary, casual or self-employed basis and three quarters were part-time . . . many did not qualify for any maternity leave, maternity pay, paid holidays, or sick pay' (Brannen and Moss, 1991: 65).

Our sample was fairly evenly divided, then, between women with professional careers and those in routine work. Experience of paid work divided sharply along this boundary, with clerical workers overwhelmingly expressing discontent with their employment and distaste for the idea of returning to it, while professional employees recorded a large measure of satisfaction.

Experience of work

Almost half of the sample found the experience of paid work overwhelmingly boring or frustrating. Nearly all of these were in low-paid routine jobs, without prospects, training or career:

I worked as a secretary, supposedly. I got good secretarial qualifications, but I ended up really just copy typing. There wasn't enough
work to do. We were expected to look busy, file our nails, tuck books
under the typewriter. It was just totally nothing, outside my concept of
work – sit around look decorative and make cups of coffee when asked,
and run errands, buy flowers for the boss's wife, and I didn't see myself
in that role at all, and I was very frustrated. So I went on to the RSA
teacher's certificate, so I would be getting to teach part time, and
hopefully getting more and more, so even at 20 I was dissatisfied with
what I was doing then and looking ahead and bettering the situation.

(Deirdre)

Geraldine 'forced' herself 'to go every morning and then clock-watched
all day'; she and Susan both tried sideways movement to make up for the
lack of promotion: 'the weeks dragged – no opportunity to get on either –
so I was always asking for transfers to different offices to try something
different.'
Several admitted disappointment with work, a mistake in leaving school,
but lacked the will or ability to reverse the situation:

As soon as I left school . . . I realized that the job that I'd taken wasn't
really what I wanted . . . I realized that it had been a mistake to give up
school . . . but there was no one I could ask . . . and I suppose pride
prevented me from admitting it, anyway at home. I had an appointment with the careers officer . . . I think it was the standard thing in
those days . . . and mentioned this when I went along but nothing
materialized . . . so I stayed in the job I'd got.

(Jean)

Part-time jobs taken up later could prove equally frustrating:

Boredom because it was so repetitive . . . factory . . . workshop . . . till
and office work just filing and writing envelopes. . . Frustrating
because . . . I was screaming inside. I knew I was capable of more than
that.

(Lesley)

Untypically, one nurse shared the frustration. She resented the health
service hierarchy. 'I experienced terrible frustration as a nurse. I . . . it . . .
it's difficult to explain. I felt like a frustrated medical student' (Joan).
Nurses otherwise were engrossed and rewarded by their work. They
were the most numerous among a group of women in professional or
semi-professional jobs who had satisfying careers. More than most, nurses
felt immersed in their work and changed by it:

It was very, very, very hard work and . . . I think it changed me. Made
me grow up quite quickly because . . . I was very, very, very immature
when I first started and, it was psychiatric nursing I did so . . . it was
very interesting so it stimulated me intellectually but it was very

emotionally demanding as well . . . my whole life was taken up in it after that.

(May)

I'd simply never been in touch with ordinary people. And when I went into nursing . . . that is the most rewarding aspect in nursing – to get contact with all sorts of people.

(Helen)

Similarly involved was one clerical worker who determined to find something interesting against the odds. 'I developed this philosophy . . . however boring the job is you are called upon to do . . . you can always make something of it . . . you've got to ask yourself how the work gets to you, where it goes to afterwards . . . how the company or the organisation works . . . just find out how everything ticks' (Val).

About a quarter of those interviewed were very positive, enjoying the intrinsic rewards of nursing or health work, or the more classic rewards of careered employment. Marjorie, in a county council trainee scheme, achieved promotion and responsibility; Iris as a children's librarian 'had a budget to spend and a couple of libraries to run so I was more or less left to get on with it – which I enjoyed doing.'

The remaining quarter had a mixed experience: different jobs bringing different rewards (for example routine work filling in time until nurse training), or work that was intrinsically satisfying (teaching) done in a difficult environment. As Alison remarked, 'They all varied. Of course, all jobs at first aren't too bad.'

For some, unrewarding work brought a measure of independence, spending power and social life:

The year I worked in an office I hated but it paid my rent and I had plenty of money to enjoy myself with. That year socially was extremely good.

(Gemma)

Indeed, the social rewards of employment were widely acknowledged. Nineteen respondents spoke of being involved – socially or otherwise. This might be a compensation for tedious work, but more often the sense of involvement accompanied more rewarding occupations.

The sample contained many women whose jobs were routine, tedious, low paid and only socially rewarding. But it also contained people who were engrossed and satisfied by their work, particularly nurses, other health workers and teachers. On the whole these women were not looking for change, so much as having change thrust upon them. As we shall see when we examine decisions about returns to education in the next chapter, typically their careers were blocked, by career breaks or by responsibilities for children. Several found that nursing, or librarianship, or radiography, could not be combined with children, or that they could only be combined on terms that devalued earlier qualifications.

A woman at work

Did being a woman affect your experience of work?

No. I was doing women's work you see.

(Felicity)

This was one of the most common answers to this question. Most women were 'doing women's work'. They thus illustrated the overwhelming importance of gender as a structural variable affecting employment. They also illustrated the more detailed point that women tend to work alongside women. But at the same time they did not feel the impact of these structural forces in their day-to-day lives. Doing women's work and working alongside women may indeed insulate women from the experience of discrimination, even while it confirms their restricted place in the job market:

> Well you see the NHS – the department I worked for employed only women, because it was to do with analysis from prescriptions. There was just a room of about a hundred women all working in there together with a superior who was a man – executive officer class I would imagine.

(Sally)

> The whole nursing hierarchy itself is pretty intimidating and there's more females in that than males so really I didn't really feel any disadvantage of being a woman.

(Joan)

Most nurses felt that as women in a woman's profession (albeit increasingly populated by men) they suffered no discrimination. Gemma, asked rather a leading question in the excerpt below, came nearest to describing the male domination of hospitals, but denied that gender was a significant feature of the experience:

> *Do you think the fact that you were a woman affected your experience of work? I mean you were in what is a female-dominated role in a male dominated medical world. Were you very conscious of that at the time?*
> Yes, I suppose I was. I didn't like the attitude of some doctors who assumed you were just there to help them. I do think doctors consider nurses as second-class citizens but that's the strange hierarchy of hospital work. Everyone is categorized – porters aren't even human beings. You just have to accept that really.
> *But was there any perception on your part that that was not only the hierarchy of medicine; that it was also the hierarchy of men and women?*
> Well, you got the same attitude from female doctors, and the senior female nursing staff, which is as bad.

Civil servants who worked alongside men were not conscious of different treatment, prospects or promotions. Sally, for example, remarked, 'I don't think there was really any difference. . . . Women were encouraged to go in for promotion boards' and Lindsay, working in a similar environment (Weights and Measures Inspectorate) felt she had the opportunity, but found that 'there was some resentment from the men'.

Some respondents recognized the existence of male domination in the hierarchy of authority, but showed no discontent with their place. Among reasons given were lack of ambition, no personal experience of discrimination and the rewards of staying at the bottom of the hierarchy:

> I think librarianship is the sort of job that attracts a lot of women but comparatively few of them reach the upper levels – this is very obvious. Most of the chief librarians and deputies were men, in fact most of the people in senior positions were men. I think what I felt about my work was that I enjoyed doing it, I was reasonably well paid but I didn't have any great ambitions to go much further.
>
> (Iris)

> I taught mainly in junior school where there were always a lot of women and so I was accepted, although headmasters tend to be headmasters, I think women are accepted as equals.
>
> (Meryl)

> I was fortunate that my head of department was a woman, which was unusual at that time. There was certainly a very definite feeling that it was difficult for me to get on . . . I didn't have any idea of wanting to move on I was quite happy with the position I was in. I think so often if you move up the scale into administration work, you lose the contact with people that I really enjoy.
>
> (Claire)

Thus women in the professions and Civil Service almost all denied personal experience of being treated differently as women. They may have been aware of structural features of women's work in their particular occupations, and some added qualifications such as men's resentment at their superior status. But their resounding answer to the question of whether or not they had personal experience of different treatment as a woman was no.

Respondents in office jobs experienced discrimination more directly and interpreted it in gendered terms. Avril, a tracer, found her career path blocked, because the next grade up was seen as 'men's work':

> Because of the boredom which came from just merely reproducing draughtsmen's work, I moved around. I worked with engineers, then I went to work for the rural district council so I worked with architects. This put an added layer of interest you see. It was different. And then, working with the architects I would go out with the building inspectors and gradually I got another dimension to the job, so what I was doing I was adding to the bit of a job that I had. I was wringing the most out of

it . . . then I moved about so much I had my own section and then I trained other would be tracers. . . . That was as far as I could go.
But were there no prospects of getting on?
Well very limited you see. The men didn't particularly mind me working with them if I stayed as a tracer but they didn't like me encroaching upon actually doing the drawings. They didn't want me to start coming into their domain.
So was tracing mainly a women's job?
Yes. And it was lower in status and in pay, enormously.

Two bank clerks remarked on the encouragement given to male employees and the speed with which they moved through the routine jobs:

> They were always encouraged to take the professional banking exams which we weren't – they were of course employed on the understanding that they would take the exams and we weren't.
>
> (Geraldine)

> In the bank I heard that the young chap who started the same day as me working there, he had less O levels and A levels than I had – there were always more women working in what they called the machine room – he was given about one or two weeks' experience of what goes on in there and then moved on to do something more interesting, higher grade work, whereas I was there for the whole nine months that I worked at that branch.
>
> (Juliet)

Alison, working in a private company, thought there was only one way to get on as a woman:

> All women were regarded as down and kept down. All the reps were men, all the managing directors were men and the only women that ever got on were those that slept with the bosses. It was the only way of getting on so that made it very unsatisfactory.

And Paula spoke of sexual harassment:

> Sometimes they would go too far and when you got cross, they would wonder why, what have we done? Generally, I think they thought that all girls whatever they did in the factory, were just theirs for pawing and mauling.

Vera, in work study, commented on pay differentials:

> I used to get cross when the men who were doing the same job as I was were getting more money, especially when I thought I was doing the job better than some of them.

Several women connected the work they did and their position in the hierarchy with other people's expectations that young girls were just filling in time before marriage. It was regarded as 'waiting time' (Rae), or 'you stayed on the shopfloor until you got married' (Moira) or 'nobody considered you might be capable of getting on – they all expected you to just work in a typing pool till you either got married or left' (Susan).

> I was very much treated as . . . I was just a temporary person in the office, and would be very soon going away to bring up children so don't worry too much about her kind of thing, she must get on with it until that stage.
>
> (Kath)

Some respondents acknowledged that gendered perceptions had limited their own horizons:

> The fact that I was a woman meant that I only just aimed for the jobs that women do part-time. And it's automatically, either an office job or a shop job . . . as a woman, I think I was very blinkered.
>
> (Lesley)

> If I'd been a bloke, maybe I'd have stayed there, I wouldn't have left to go and travel abroad.
>
> (Gwen)

What respondents had taken for granted and accepted on leaving school might no longer be acceptable. Miriam commented, 'I took a woman's place, as I was expected to at the time. I've very different views now, of course.' Yvonne, trained as a nursery nurse, described it as 'all women. It was a women's college. It was job that was traditionally done by women. I hadn't really thought about it. I mean now I would think it had [affected experience of work]. At the time I didn't.'

Experience of work, then, was quite sharply divided between those with professional careers and those in routine work. The former for the most part found their work engrossing and rewarding; and while they acknowledged some features of the gender hierarchy at work, they denied that being a woman had been a disadvantage to themselves. They enjoyed their work, felt no discrimination, and there was no mention of sexual harassment.

The experience of women in routine work was more painful. They not only suffered a large measure of boredom and frustration, but also were very conscious of discriminatory sponsoring and promotion procedures and of differences in pay. Their experiences as women at work were described in more directly gendered terms, with sexual relations and harassment on the one hand and limits imposed by perceptions about marriage and motherhood on the other.

Women in these two categories appeared in our sample in almost equal numbers. While their experiences of paid work in the past were diverse, they shared much more common ground in the present. With few exceptions (mainly among teachers) their position in the job market – now combined with their position as mothers, wives and housewives – was fragile.

Private careers – wives, housewives and mothers

Our respondents grew up (though with some allowances for differences in age) with the expectations that wife, mother and housewife were the proper female roles and source of women's identity. Very high rates of marriage prevailed during their adolescence; cohabitation was not yet widely acceptable; women continued to bear the major responsibility for housework; most women had at least one child; and most women left the labour market when children were born. Most respondents did, in fact, conform to these expectations and experience all three roles.

Marriage

> Young girls are, from a very early age, socialized and encouraged to see their future, their career, as lying in marriage.
>
> (Gittins, 1985: 77)

> Women continue ... to be economically dependent on both a marriage market and a labour market. In both they are disadvantaged economically.
>
> (ibid.: 78)

These claims about women and marriage – about marriage as a career, the centre of women's lives, and about women's economic relation to marriage – suggest that women's position in marriage will be at least as important as their position in the labour market in understanding their decisions about education. If marriage is a career, then decisions about marriage and public careers will be entwined. And if women are disadvantaged economically in both marriage and labour markets then returning to higher education may be understood as an attempt to redress the balance in either sphere or both.

We asked about expectations and experience of marriage with two key ideas in mind. The first was to look at the part marriage played in early career decisions and ask to what extent expectations about marriage – and marriage itself – had stood in the way of a public career. The other was the extent to which the experience of marriage exposed women to the need for developing a new career at a later stage. We therefore asked our respondents to look back to their younger expectations of marriage, and to their subsequent experience.

Our sample were typical of the general population of women of their age, in the large part that marriage had played in their lives. Most had been married at least once (41 out of 43), and four of them two or three times. For the other two marriage simply had not happened. As May put it, 'I just didn't get married I suppose because I didn't meet anybody I wanted to marry and that was it.'

There was no one in the sample, then, who had clearly chosen not to marry. There were some who made their choice to marry within constraints that they resented, at the time or later. It was a minority who described pressures from outside as playing a large part in their decision to marry but these may well be relevant to others. There were very tangible pressures in the case of early pregnancy. 'I didn't want to get married – I was pressurized into it by all concerned' (Geraldine).

Deirdre spoke of more general social pressures:

In those days the permissive society hadn't reached Yorkshire, and living together was really a bit, well, you had to be very brave to do it and I wasn't at 19 able to resist those pressures of parents and friends. I don't see the necessity for it now and I think an 18- or 19-year-old coming up now wouldn't see the necessity.

Marilyn saw marriage as a way of extricating herself from existing family commitments, a traditional escape route for young women from their family of origin. 'I think that without even realizing it I got married to escape from looking after the children.'

Gemma was rather exceptional in putting career first. 'I wasn't bothered at all whether I got married or not . . . I just then concerned myself with how I was going to support myself and how I was going to buy myself a house and practical problems like that.'

The other kind of expectation that our respondents discussed was about the nature of marriage. As girls, had they accepted romantic ideas of marriage current in popular literature, did they expect it to solve all life's problems – emotional, social and economic? If marriage is seen as a career in itself, then careers in paid work may be relegated to secondary importance; and secondary decisions may be put off until primary ones are settled. Marriage may then be seen as standing in the way of a plan for future life and career. Girls adopting these ideas might opt to leave school early, focus on early earnings, be content to stay on the bottom of the work ladder and marry early.

Such a scenario provides a variety of reasons for women to give up education in their early years, and then to take it up again when the inadequacy of their preparation for key aspects of adult life becomes plain. We were interested in the extent to which our respondents would identify with aspects of this scenario or deny being seduced by popular imagery.

Some of our respondents, described above, married out of hard social pressure as much as out of soft romantic notions. But a large number of our respondents did identify with the scenario of romantic illusion. Martha, for example, admitted, 'I think I thought that marriage would be the answer to all the things that were wrong. You soon realize it isn't.' Barbara contrasted past and present perceptions, 'I got married really, not through parental pressure, or my aunt's pressure, because at the time I suppose it was a romantic notion. But now I think there's only tax reasons involved.'

Expectations of marriage, then, had a certain uniformity. With few exceptions, girls had assumed that they would marry and had carried that assumption through into practice. There was also widespread acknowledgement of some seduction by romantic illusions about the way marriage would solve life's problems. Experience of marriage was much more varied. We interviewed people who expressed contentment with marriage, as well as those in the various bitter throes of separation and divorce, and some who had come through the other side to a measure of contented independence. The romantic illusion scenario suggests that disillusion may not be far round the corner:

> The development of ideals of romance and romantic love in contemporary society has been so strongly all-pervasive that few people are fully aware of the bitter pill beneath the sugar coating in marriage. . . Undoubtedly this imbalance between ideal and reality contributes markedly to so much disillusionment, suffering and divorce. Contemporary ideology of the family presents marriage as an equal partnership between a man and a woman who love each other. In reality, the social, political and economic structures of modern industrial society are such that only in the rarest of cases can marriage ever be equal.
>
> (Gittins, 1985: 90)

Most of our respondents acknowledged that experience brought some change of perspective about marriage. One put expectation and reality the opposite way round to Gittins:

> Marriage was a lot, lot better and a lot safer and a lot happier than I thought it was going to be. I was amazed at the status you get when you become married. You know, the postman delivers a letter to your house through your front door . . . I was quite incredulous. I think I treated it as a bit of a game of playing at house in a way . . . but I think maybe a lot of newly-married people do that.
>
> (Val)

A number, such as Avril and Belinda, described marriages that had lived up to expectations:

> When I got married it was because Mike and I always got on very, very well together. You know we . . . he's still my best friend and I feel that I'm still his best friend, you know, and so we supported one another and I think since we got married we've got more out of life because he in a sense was very similar to myself.
>
> (Avril)

But the illusion/disillusion scenario was supported to some degree by those still married, as well as more bitterly by those who had separated or divorced. Some emphasized the emotional work:

I was prepared practically – I knew how to cook and clean and run round other people, but the emotional – the give and take of marriage – the compromise – I wasn't prepared for that at all.

(Lesley)

Now I can see that it's not about romantic idealized love-matches that go on for ever. It's about friendship, practicalities, understanding each other and it's really, it's something that you work at rather than go into and sit back and let it happen.

(Marjorie)

Others focused on the practical:

I was very undomesticated. I never had to do anything in the way of cooking or cleaning. And that was a bit of a shock. Especially when I was at work and I had to come home to all that. That took time to adjust to.

(Jenny)

Lesley focused on the economic and social realities of a marriage commitment. 'I don't see any other system could work so well for bringing children up . . . But I can see that so many people are caught up. It's very difficult to get out of – especially for a woman who's tied down with children.'

But the eleven who had separated or divorced felt the full force of disillusion. For them marriage did not solve life's problems. Rather, it left them exposed, emotionally, socially and economically. Since most had children they were left with a need to support themselves and their dependants, often with inadequate qualifications and work experience:

There's no security in marriage itself. I've had two husbands . . . one left me and I left the other. I don't think it gives you security with a child.

(Cathy)

At a later stage in the interview, several connect their decisions about returning to education with the economic impact of separation or divorce. While education and career do not appear as an alternative to marriage in these women's accounts of their early lives, they become exactly that when marriage breaks down.

Marriage seen as a career is a form of employment in which women are dependent on men. Men's better access to the labour market, and women's role in unpaid work, together mean that most women accept a degree of dependence in marriage. However, like women in general, a high proportion of our respondents found that marriage did not provide the kind of economic support expected from the traditional male family wage. There were the two who didn't marry – because it didn't happen, rather than because they didn't expect or want it. Some had periods of supporting husbands, or married men who earned low wages. Rather more (11) experienced separation and/or divorce, some more than once.

Part of the difference between this reality and the male breadwinner model of family life can be explained by general social changes that have come about during the period of our respondents' adult lives. The increase in married women's employment, with shorter breaks for childcare, and the increase in divorce and separation, are likely to mean that paid employment has played a much larger role in their lives than in their youthful imaginations. While none of our respondents could be said to have found a career in marriage, the idea of marriage as a career in itself has been cast into doubt in a much wider arena than the one we are describing.

Housewives?

What is a housewife? We and our respondents found it difficult to define. Asked rather naively about periods as full-time housewives, our respondents gave answers based on a range of different assumptions. Two described themselves as housewives when they gave up paid work on account of sickness or moving (but did not have children). Others rejected the label on the grounds that they always had occupation other than housework, such as part-time employment or study. It was difficult to determine where the boundaries lay between being employed, unemployed, sick, student and housewife. In practice, many women in our sample had spent years in a patchwork of part-time work, courses, and being a 'housewife', often simultaneously.

We therefore classified people as having been full-time housewives if their other activities were at least nominally part time. In the end, eight women were classified as never having been full-time housewives. These were mainly the two who had not married and those who had not had children. But there were more for whom being a housewife was a very temporary state of affairs plugging gaps in rather more full-time careers. Being a full-time housewife went with having children (34 women in the sample had had children) or occasionally with sickness or unemployment (2). But there were a few who had children and continued full-time employment, virtually without break. There were also some who would have children – and perhaps become housewives – in the future. The respondents then do not fall neatly into 'housewives' and 'career women'. The sample contains clear examples of both, but more who have mingled paid and unpaid work. The majority have some experience of being full-time housewives, but the number who have never been full-time housewives is much larger than those who have never had full-time paid employment.

We asked about the social aspects of 'being a housewife' rather than about the housework, and our respondents discussed the experience mainly in terms of isolation or social relationships, and occasionally in terms of social status. The labour of housework was never far away, in the limits it imposed, or the scope it gave for friendships. Questions of the division of labour lurked beneath some women's accounts.

Of the 34 who had been full-time housewives, a rather small minority (5) spoke in terms that were wholly or predominantly positive. In particular, some found the time and opportunity to make friends that they had otherwise missed. Moira recorded that 'it was only when I was a housewife and the children came that I was able to sit down and make friends, and I have kept them', and Lindsay described the rewards of 'sharing the experiences that you have with other women and with your family'. Rhona was perhaps the most enthusiastic:

> When the children were little and I was at home being a housewife, I loved it. . . . Living next door to me was a girl who I am still best friends with . . . I think you're lucky if you make that sort of friendship ever in your lifetime.

But a full half assessed their experience in terms that were wholly or predominantly negative. The main themes were social isolation, depression, low social status and resentment about the division of labour. Juliet echoed the academic literature, which associates motherhood of small children with depression (Brown and Harris, 1978), 'I did feel isolated, when the children were very small and I was depressed mentally so that made me feel bored and more isolated.' Sally was taken by surprise. 'I must admit I did look forward to it. And it was such an isolating experience that it was having a very bad effect on me.'

Resentment at the division of labour underlay some experiences:

> I absolutely hated it and very soon I was so resentful of everything – staying at home doing cleaning, cooking, etc; I just wanted to get out and do things but my husband wouldn't let me outside the door – so that probably made it ten times worse.
>
> (Geraldine)

Belinda remarked on the difference between being a housewife and doing housework for herself. 'I think now, yes, [it can be rewarding] because there are so many ways in which I can occupy myself and I'm doing it for me but I found the demands before were a bit unpleasant.'

Helen's remark about the social status of being a housewife speaks for several others. 'A housewife is looked upon as you are so dud, you are not capable of anything else.'

The remainder (11) balanced the rewards and the pains. They enjoyed it as a temporary phase, or by contrast, found that it improved as their social networks grew. Moving house or living in a flat could exacerbate isolation for a period. A few spoke of the need to make it work, to act positively to counter isolation; and people used the space it gave to develop interests and social activities:

At the time it fulfilled a need in me. I wanted to be at home with my children, and I enjoyed it. But after two years – I'd had enough. I had another need. So if you asked me if I would be a full-time housewife – no, it wouldn't be rewarding at all, in fact it would destroy me.

(Marjorie)

Susan was most eloquent about the inadequacy of the housewife role as an identity. She encapsulated many of the themes addressed by other respondents in her account of the mixed pleasures and pains of doing housework with the much less enticing business of being a housewife:

I enjoyed that, when I'd got small children because I liked baking and I liked cleaning and cooking . . . but what really grieved me was being told that that was all I could do – it was what I was supposed to do and I shouldn't want anything more. You can enjoy being a housewife but that doesn't mean that you are just a housewife. I thought I'm a person as well, I also like reading books, dancing – I shouldn't be told that you can do that all day and nothing else so why should I be told that I'd got to be a housewife for the rest of my life. I didn't actually resent it but I didn't see it as the most important purpose in life.

Thus while a number of our sample had found short-term pleasures in being a housewife, the majority had not found the role worthy of a long-term career or source of identity. The length of the short term varied greatly. Some measured contentment in years, whereas for others six months was the limit. But nearly all described this as a phase rather than a life's work.

Motherhood

Motherhood had brought the expected rewards in most cases. Our respondents had found pleasure in their children, even if it was sometimes mixed with anguish and frustration. There was little sense of education as being an escape from this role, though there was some sense of it as an alternative when motherhood didn't happen, or when its temporariness as a consuming occupation became clear.

Not all had had children. For some this was a temporary phase, but the two unmarried respondents were beginning to acknowledge that their futures might be without motherhood, and others' expectations of having children were faltering. One woman whose five-year-old daughter had chosen to live with her father, experienced this painful personal catastrophe as a rejection of her as a mother. Like marriage, then, motherhood was not always predictable. More of our respondents were without children by accident than by design.

There were unplanned pregnancies, too. In one case this had interrupted a career that might otherwise have happened; in another it had resulted in an unsuccessful marriage. There were, then, women who found a large space where motherhood might have been; women for whom motherhood led to the interruption of the usual sources of economic support (career or marriage); and some for whom single parenthood meant a need for increased income. Thus a number of circumstances surrounding motherhood pushed women away from the role of full-time mother.

Most of our respondents had accepted at least some aspects of the social role of mother along with biological parenthood. Most had periods without full-time employment. All accepted the obligations of motherhood, as it is presently constructed, taking major responsibility for the day-to-day care of young children, without expecting significant contribution from the other parent.

A few made comments about motherhood that were almost entirely negative. Geraldine, for example, acknowledged, 'I don't see my children as the centrepiece of my life . . . Motherhood was never very rewarding for me at all really.' Paula seemed more overcome by the difficulties than the delights:

> Not satisfying, I find it really hard work. I had a difficult first baby, one that cries day and night and nobody finds anything wrong with him, just said cuddle him, and I usually found I was falling to sleep peeling the potatoes . . . Frustrating, yes, very, not being able to do what you wanted, you were ruled by babies the whole time.

At the other extreme were women whose answers were wholly enthusiastic:

> I thought that was magical. I really liked that. . . It's about the most worthwhile thing I've ever accidentally done in my life. . . I had worried about how my head would stand up to it, but I just adopted the viewpoint that here was another human being who couldn't feed herself or clean herself and just needed you, and it was just nice to be needed by somebody that belonged to you. Yes, it was a good experience.
>
> (Val)

More characteristic was the mixture of rewards and frustrations. Boulton's distinction between the short term (often characterized by frustration, exhaustion and irritation, and the long term (in which the rewards may be more evident) is useful for our respondents too (Boulton, 1983):

> I've loved having the children and enjoyed that side of it – they've been rewarding – but it's the frustrations of wet washing, etc. that can get on top of you.
>
> (Janet)

> It's been very mixed. It's been tremendously exciting, fascinating, it's been rewarding and it's been full of emotional upsets, very traumatic,

physically exhausting initially as well but I wouldn't not have children for all the world.

(Joan)

Some took pleasure in certain stages ('You enjoy them when they are babies' or 'I get satisfaction when I see the children now'), but found their overall experience less joyful. Transience was a common theme:

I enjoyed the whole experience of being a housewife and a mother – even childbirth was a marvellous experience. I did find, after a while – two to three years, I began to feel as though I was vegetating so I started to look for outlets – I went to night school.

(Joanne)

The overall picture was of women who enjoyed their children, but who found aspects of the role of motherhood variously stressful or painful. Even for the most enthusiastic, their absorption in the role of caring for children was limited – if only by the passage of time. The women who talked of the need for something else expressed this most clearly:

For one section of my life, yes, for one part of it, but not totally fulfilling.

(Gwen)

I enjoyed my job as a mother, my role as a mother but I wanted something else as well.

(Jean)

Conclusion

Wife, housewife, mother are all proposed as careers for women and as identities. Being a housewife is more than doing the housework, being a mother more than bearing children. Women are expected to find fulfilment in these roles, often as alternatives to a public career. Indeed they are seen as more embracing than a public career in their fusion of personal identity and useful work.

But these ideas are strongly contradicted by our respondents. Nearly all had tried marriage, housewife and motherhood roles; and all were looking for something else. On balance, motherhood had been the most rewarding of the three. The rub here, though, was the limit on this source of identity in a period of low family size and limited jurisdiction over the lives of their children. The majority who enjoyed their children soon found the need for something else.

Our respondents varied in the amount of pleasure they had been able to extract from these roles. But they were unanimous in feeling the inadequacy of domesticity as a life's work and source of identity.

If domesticity had turned out fatally flawed as a career, then what of more public careers? Both main groups of employees – in routine jobs and in professions – were handicapped by the way women's public careers have been subordinated to their domestic ones. Those in routine jobs had not seen the need for a career for themselves, or had felt trapped by discriminatory attitudes and practices deriving especially from expectations that marriage and children would be their career. Women in 'women's careers' felt unable to combine them with motherhood. Both groups now faced a need for work that would be personally and economically rewarding. Divorced and separated women suffered those pressures more acutely, but married women also felt under strong pressure to contribute to the family income.

4

Decisions

From the context of family and career circumstances we moved to more direct questions about the decision to return to education. We asked for respondents' own assessment of precipitating factors, external changes and what they wanted to change in their lives. We asked how much they felt it was part of a plan, or whether on the contrary they felt they drifted into it; and why they chose this path rather than any other that might have been available.

Most could identify one or two key precipitating factors. Most frequently these were family-based (33), and by far the most common single factor was decreasing demands from children. Usually, the point at which this happened was the youngest child starting school or play-group. There was another group (6) for whom marriage breakdown provided the catalyst. On the other hand, factors connected with work played a significant part in these accounts, ten women pointing to work as the main factor. Economic reasons (4) and mental health (3) also played this part, with education seen as the resolution to financial or personal crisis.

What emerged strikingly from the interviews was the way that elements merged together. Women pointed to a particular decisive factor, but described it against a background of possibilities and impossibilities, jobs, lack of qualifications, children growing up, but still needing care, and so on. One seemed to say this directly, when she said that it 'would probably have happened anyway'. Others recognized it in the intricate web of elements that they went on to describe:

> Lots of things really I suppose. First, apart from the way I felt that I wanted to get back in – sort of prepare the future – I didn't want to be stuck behind a till in a shop. My husband was going through quite a bad experience with his work – well he almost had a nervous breakdown. He's in a manual occupation – he was working continental shifts, which meant that he had very few weekends off. Our family life was really nil. He very rarely saw the children. I just thought we can't go on like this,

so he changed his occupation. He took a great drop in money, which meant we were really struggling. I thought I can't see us being like this for the rest of our lives. I've got the opportunity to do something, so that eventually if he's ever out of work at least, hopefully, there will be one decent wage coming in to the house. So that was one thing . . . my daughter had started school. My son was then nearly three. I thought if you don't start doing something now, you never will. Plus, my son has had a great deal of developmental difficulty . . . I was getting over-anxious about him . . . but I think the main reason was that my husband was in such a poor occupation – I really needed to do something.

(Lesley)

Barbara, who started decisively with her husband's achievement of financial security, added a collection of other points. 'My husband, that's the only reason . . . it was purely financial, and the fact that I'd finished work . . . I couldn't see myself having any children . . . I was depressed working in an office. Higher education was the only thing I actually wanted to do.'

Rhona who was on a teaching course described her decision like this:

The youngest one started school so from that point of view I was looking towards the future when I could return to work full time. There's no way that you can go back full time in nursing with a family – except into jobs like health visiting or clinic work – otherwise the hours are so irregular that they just don't fit into family life. I had considered health visiting but mostly what changed my mind was that we lived in Hong Kong for two years. I couldn't work out there on a part-time basis. There were so many nurses out there who were married to civil engineers that they could pick and choose, so I ran play school instead, and when I came back I helped in school.

These complex factors reflect complex lives, in which economic issues, job prospects, family responsibilities, changes in marriage and mother-hood are all put in the balance for a major decision. For some education may seem the only way of diminishing the restrictions of circumstance; for others a variety of circumstances needs to fall into place before education can be considered. In this respect our students resembled women adult students in McLaren's study, most of whom 'had to take several important factors, such as money, their work, or their educational and occupational opportunities, into account, not just their family circumstances' (McLaren, 1985: 90).

The way these decisions emerge from a network of elements also suggests the dominance of outside circumstance over personal purpose. The decisions seem over-determined, in their dependence on a complex web of circumstances being right. Issues of planning and of contingency arise throughout these interviews, and we develop this discussion further at the end of the chapter.

Family reasons

Childcare

A very high proportion of respondents (23) spoke of children growing up as an element in their decision and 16 spoke of it as the key element. These large numbers reflect the ages of the sample, and of the wider population of mature students, with its preponderance of younger adults. They also reflect patterns of motherhood in the wider society and the extent to which women perceived parenting as a central role – with their personal lives to be thought of after the most pressing demands of young children.

The sheer extent of women's lives after children was noted long ago in Titmuss' account of changes in family life (Titmuss, 1958), but the obvious fact is easier to deal with as a sociologist than as a young girl leaving school, or as a mother with young children. Many of our respondents convey a sense of being unprepared, as if marriage and motherhood constituted a barrier to thinking beyond small children. This may reflect the time and energy absorbing character of infant care; also, perhaps, the uncertainties about such events; and perhaps, too, an imaginative difficulty for younger women in grasping the realities of child-rearing and perceiving the terrain beyond. More general social change, in which women's experiences are rather different from those prevailing as they grew up, may also lie behind this sense of lack of preparation.

Many of our respondents spoke as if they were beginning to plan their own lives for the first time; and often as if this were a painful experience:

> Well I suppose I put off thinking about the future. As you know, when they are tiny and they are so demanding . . . you are like a little machine till the end of the day and I did enjoy it but at the back of my mind I knew that when they did sort of start to become independent, or the need to do something else came – I mean I love kids but they keep growing up, and you can't keep having them.
>
> (Helen)

> I'm 32 now and I've perhaps nearly another 30 years of work . . . I suppose I did in a sense feel that I should do something now with my life.
>
> (Lindsay)

The parents in our sample were pre-occupied with selfishness and selflessness. Most subscribed to an ideal of motherhood in which their prime duty and purpose in life was to care for their children (even if they were less single-minded about wifehood and housewifery) (Riley, 1983). They accepted the caring role as a significant source of identity for themselves (Graham, 1983). As in other studies of mothers (Boulton, 1983) (and with one notable exception) they accepted the task of parenting as belonging to them rather than to their partners. So they felt their lives had been centred on children and that children's interests continued to be paramount. For those in economic distress the desire for higher education could easily be legitimated in terms of the needs of the family. For others, there was often a sense of unease about putting their own lives first:

I don't mean that the children didn't need me any more but in a sense it would have been wrong for me to need them too much – to make my life out of them.

(Lesley)

The role of being a wife, a mother or a daughter couldn't be all that your life was about. Your life had to be about yourself and that has been the biggest change because once you have made a conscious decision to get more out of life for yourself you end up by giving more to others as well which is a good thing.

(Sally)

I suppose my identity was through the children, I was somebody's mother and somebody's wife, which I didn't mind for a while, because I thoroughly enjoyed the mother role and everything. But I suppose it was facing up at the end of the day that there was a me somewhere inside it all and I'd got to do something about it.

(Heather)

For a few, there was more sense of a plan for their own future, of a lying in wait until the moment was right to take up an education that they had long intended. For these, the children growing to some measure of independence was seen as the first possible time for implementing the project:

Not because the children were growing up, but I was waiting for the children to grow up, so that I could come and do something.

(Jean)

When the children were both at an age when I could go into education I did. I'd thought about doing it for a long time.

(Kath)

On a more practical level (and rather as a side issue) a number remarked that education fitted better with the continuing demands of young children than a job would have done. Six explained that their children still needed them, and others made the same assumptions. These women took to themselves the constraints of the school day and found a kind of convenience in the education world. Kath 'wanted something that would fit in with school hours and higher education does that. Jobs don't.' Respondents reflected the general pattern among women with growing children of returning to the public world, but with reduced commitment (Martin and Roberts, 1984):

> I considered a full-time job but that was rejected because of the fact of the age of the children – that they were too young and also I would've felt very guilty about going to work.
>
> (Marjorie)

> I suppose the big change was when my son started school – I decided that I didn't particularly want to work full time as the children were still fairly young and needed me. It is very difficult to get part-time work in librarianship.
>
> (Isabel)

The predominant feeling expressed by these mothers was that children growing up exposed the inadequacy of a life experienced through motherhood. The experience had not for the most part let them down; but it had proved transient. It demanded everything of them and then left them painfully exposed. Some women woke up when the last child started school with no qualifications for worthwhile or remunerative work, or with qualifications that they now found they could not use. They continued to accept the mother role (which severely constrained their choices) but also had to accept that motherhood would no longer be an absorbing occupation or a sufficient source of identity.

The growing up of the children also exposed women to new questions about 'being a housewife'. A role that might satisfy while combined with bringing up small children could look very different as a life's work and central source of identity. Thus Janet spoke of 'the monotony – especially once the children were at play school – there wasn't enough to occupy me here'.

A large proportion of those among the sample who were married expressed a strong desire to escape from being a housewife (14), seeing this as an aspect of their decision to seek higher education. Their remarks about the housewife role were entirely conventional, and might have been borrowed from Gavron (1966) or Oakley (1974), though most, like Lesley, were careful to detach discontent from their children. 'I didn't want to escape from my children as such, but I wanted to escape from the routine of it all.' Martha spoke for many in describing her sense of the emptiness of the housewife role:

> After the first couple of years I realized that I wasn't a housewife. And I suppose like a lot of women I thought why? You know everyone else is busily doing their housework . . . they all seem quite happy, so why aren't I? But I wouldn't call it escape really. They can co-exist. I didn't want to get rid of one to do the other. I just wanted a bit more out of life.

There were some variations in the by now conventional message. Cathy acknowledged that her course protected her from the demands of family and was becoming anxious about it coming to an end. 'Now I dread leaving because in a way my children's expectations are that I will become a housewife again and that frightens me.' Marjorie's critique referred to the now characteristic blend of roles, 'children and domesticity and a list of part-time jobs just hadn't fulfilled me'.

There was the occasional dissenting voice, such as Vera who felt under economic pressure to develop her career. 'I'd got quite a wide circle of friends and I think I could have made quite a nice life if I'd had to.'

But most of the still-married mothers in our sample were reluctant housewives, pushing that role as far to the margins of their lives as possible. While children were young they did part-time jobs, voluntary work – especially in schools and playgroups – and courses in FE colleges. When they thought children were old enough some wasted no time:

> The first time I could have come was the year I came here. That was the very first time that the children were old enough I thought to leave and I fulfilled my duty with them. My husband was on his feet and I had got the relevant qualifications and that was the very first time.
>
> (Avril)

Others found thinking about the time after children harder, and were more painfully aware that the housewife role could not continue satisfactorily as the children grew more independent:

> I suppose it was just something niggling at the back of my mind which as long as I could put off having to face it, then I did do.
>
> (Heather)

Marriage breakdown

Eight women mentioned marriage breakdown in their discussions of precipitating factors in their decision to take up higher education, and six of these saw it as the prime one. The economic realities of marriage and motherhood were borne in on these women when husbands left or ceased offering economic support:

> In the first place I needed to increase my earning power, so that I could earn enough to keep myself and my daughter.
>
> (Val)

> I think the main thing was that my husband went out and had an affair – there was absolutely nothing I could do about it – I had no money – then I felt I didn't have any prospects of getting a job other than a factory job – I had two small children – living out in the middle of nowhere – and I was extremely outraged – so I decided then that I was going to work but there was just nothing around.
>
> (Geraldine)

Where marriages had broken, motherhood exposed the need for secure employment especially harshly. Studies of women and poverty show clearly how vulnerable are single mothers (Glendinning and Millar, 1987/92) and how difficult it is to escape the trap set between benefits and employment practices (Brown, 1989). This group of respondents saw education in very practical terms as a way of developing a career and increasing earning power.

Separation and divorce could also leave a personal and social void, making the customary pattern of part-time work, childcare and being a housewife less attractive:

> For me I think it was being on my own and realizing that when my children left home a part-time job wasn't going to be satisfying enough and I must develop myself and really immerse myself in something that would take all my concentration, because my social life was a bit thin at the time and so that's why I decided to take the plunge.
>
> (Dorcas)

> I was looking for a whole way of life, not just a temporary job.
>
> (Val)

In one case, the finalization of divorce was a key factor 'Because he couldn't stop me' (Alison). The significance of husbands' permission was remarked upon more positively by women who had had every support, a point that is developed below.

Careers

If family issues played a large part in these discussions, so did paid work. A very large number (21) spoke of the need for a new job or career. Some of these felt trapped in unrewarding part-time jobs; others described a career that they could not combine with motherhood. Some respondents spoke more conventionally of career advancement.

Even for this last group, who were mostly women without children, gender was a feature of most of the situations they described. For example, those who had entered female-dominated professions could find their paths blocked through lack of educational qualifications:

> Only having O levels I couldn't go on to nurse teaching or health visiting because you need educational qualifications. You see these were the only two aspects of nursing that I felt I wanted to pursue, so I decided to do education full time . . . still with a view to doing these courses and staying in nursing.
>
> (May)

I was in residential work and the thing was I decided, once I'd been in residential work for about a year and a half that I wanted to do my CQSW or some kind of qualification.

(Joy)

Those who had left jobs to look after children faced a variety of situations. Moira had hoped to return to her old job, but found at first that there were no vacancies because of government cuts. Helen found that combining paid work and small children could result in demotion to insecure or less interesting work:

I'd run a ward for several years, taught the student nurses, and managed the ward – which is very rewarding – your own thing – some influence. That had replaced an academic career – management – and I think that was taken away from me when I worked part time. I just filled in.

(Helen)

It is very difficult to get part-time work in librarianship . . . Really the difficulty I could see with working full time and having children, was not having school holidays, etc.; and I could see that part-time jobs were few and far between, and although I could have continued doing part time, I couldn't see that there was going to be much future in it. You are on the minimum salary and once the job was finished, it is goodbye until they need you again. You couldn't really settle to anything in your own life.

(Isabel)

Michelle spoke eloquently about the loss of credit for experience:

Despite the fact that I enjoyed doing what I was doing when I worked full time it didn't leave me with any legacy as it were to pick up later on in life and the internal exams that you take don't count for anything else . . . even if you had returned to the Civil Service they like you to start at the step below and I'd have had to go through the whole thing again and I couldn't face that, so it left me with nothing, no qualifications, no experience that counted for much.

A number of these women seemed to be describing occupations that drew particularly upon young female school-leavers, with jobs structured on the expectation of a short working life, stopping at childbirth. The hierarchy was then reserved for the minority who remained – and the traditional expectation might be that they remained single or at least childless. Older women hoping to return to such occupations were expected to pay a price in terms of availability of suitable jobs, or of demotion into less responsible areas.

Some who had had less rewarding jobs before children were emphatic about the need for radical change. The tedium of their earlier jobs is not, of course, peculiar to women, though it is typical of a high proportion of women's jobs. The low-pay and poor conditions of the service work available part time to women with childcare responsibilities are also well documented (Beechey, 1987; Martin and Roberts, 1984).

There were lots of problems getting a job without any qualifications . . . a job that I wanted . . . I mean I wanted a career rather than a job I suppose that's what I'm saying. But to get into anything without qualifications was a non-starter anyway, plus the children.

(Kath)

Those in a stronger financial position could make more positive use of their broken work pattern; there was something in their position as mothers of young children that they could now exploit. There was a chance to rethink, an expectation that husbands could continue to offer economic support and an in-between period when full-time work would still be difficult:

When the children were quite small and I become involved in the play groups, etc., I realized that I would like to teach . . . I'd had a taste of clerical work years back and I couldn't see myself returning, I mean, I've a long time to work.

(Lindsay)

I had seven months in the civil service, which bored me to tears again, and I realized that if I'd got to work for the next 20 years I can't go back to an office job.

(Martha)

Rhona made an explicit contrast with married men, describing the flexibility for women in her position, 'I think women are often in a more fortunate position than men because they can make this change whereas the husband maybe thinks about it but he would have to go back a very long way in salary, etc. to make a change.' However, Vera's experience was of using more flexible work patterns to the advantage of both partners. 'The fact that my husband wants to work for himself, that had been in the back of our minds for some time that I should work so that he could leave work.'

While families figured largely in women's discussion of rethinking working careers, work crises also played their part. Marilyn commented that it was 'being made redundant that put me towards education' and Penelope described a downgrading of her job brought about by computerization.

These discussions took place against a background of rapidly changing working practices for women (Beechey, 1987; Martin and Roberts, 1984). Our respondents may have been born into a post-war period of domestic ideals, which proposed that mothers of young children did not do paid work; but they grew into a world of increasing women's paid employment and ideological uncertainty. Many seemed to feel the inadequacy of their preparation for paid employment; lack of educational qualifications affected career nurses and teachers as well as those who left mundane jobs to fulfil their ideals of motherhood. There were certainly a few respondents who saw a period of higher education as a break from employment, a chance to stop and reassess; but the need for better employment prospects figured very largely in most accounts.

Ideological uncertainty was resolved for most of those who had children by the solution of putting children first, while responding to a barrage of pressures to enter the labour market. For those who were mothers especially, decisions about paid work interleaved with decisions about the family, and were contingent on perceptions of family needs. Needing a new job or career vied with children growing up as a key element in the decision to embark upon higher education. Together these reasons suggest how women resolved the contradictory pressures – children first, career later.

Economic reasons

For some, though, economic pressures threw the elements into a different relationship. Low incomes and family breakdown could put the domestic ideal of motherhood into the shade in favour of a new model – mother as breadwinner. In this case career and the children's needs were more easily reconciled. A career would keep the children out of poverty.

The minority who spoke directly about economic factors in their decision were concerned with supporting themselves, their children or their families. Low incomes, marriage breakdown and in one case ageing, all demonstrated the inadequacy of the male breadwinner model of family life and put careers high on women's agenda.

Marriage breakdown has already been described as a significant precipitating factor; together with cuts in her part-time job it forced Cathy into a decision she had been putting off. 'I wanted to do it before then but I didn't have the nerve. It was that or get a full-time job and I did actually go round for a full-time job as a cleaner and didn't get it. And I was appalled at the hours and the low pay.'

But it was not only the divorced and separated who needed earnings to support the family. Women with husbands in low-paid manual jobs felt this pressure acutely, and saw their own educational capital as their key potential resource. Both Lesley and Kath felt the insecurity and the responsibility that fell to them:

> The work my husband does and did is very unstable . . . so I think there came a stage when I thought I've got to take the situation into my own hands . . . It's no use sitting back waiting for my husband to do something. He simply couldn't.

(Kath)

Lindsay described the economic pressures on women to earn in a more general way. 'The days of families coping with one wage packet are gone and I realized that it was an economic necessity that I should do something.'

Even where traditional patterns had worked so far there could be reason to fear the future:

> I've always had in the back of my mind that I did need to be potentially independent. . . especially coming towards 50, I know so many women who are my age who have been left alone in the world for one reason or another who have not been independent; and I felt that if I could stand on my own feet then I would be doing everybody, including my family, a service.

> (Belinda)

Thus the crisis of marriage breakdown threw women's economic predicament into sharp relief, but the insecurities of economic dependence were more widely apparent.

The other ways that economic factors appeared were as constraint and opportunity. Five women in our small sample remarked that this was the first time they could afford higher education. For example, Avril had paid the mortgage while her husband had done his degree, and then waited until he was established.

Support

A number of our respondents mentioned the support of family as a key factor in their decision, and particularly the support of husbands. Some spoke warmly of encouragement when confidence might otherwise have failed. Asked about any change in family circumstances Rae remarked 'getting married and I had my husband's encouragement. It was something I'd been thinking about for a long time and he just gave me the push in the right direction. Otherwise I don't think I could have done it on my own.'

Others described negotiation and balancing each others' interests:

> Ivan said it's silly going back to work unless you are doing something you like, and he felt he couldn't give up his work if I wasn't doing something I liked, or he would have felt guilty. So in order to do that, I'd got to get a bit further in education.

> (Vera)

Others mentioned the financial support of a husband with a secure income:

> I was getting older and more financially stable as well – because I'd got a husband who was looking after me and we weren't really poor – that gave me the confidence to go ahead and do it.

> (Susan)

The gratitude in these remarks may suggest something that could not be taken for granted. The two respondents above who volunteered that they could not have done without their husbands' support raise a question about women's need for permission from the men they live with. The respondent whose divorce meant that her husband could no longer stop her from going to university makes the obvious point that permission is not always given. Morgan is plainly sceptical of her respondents' comments in this area, since they consistently attribute difficulties to other people (Morgan, 1981: 39).

Planning the future

Our respondents perceived the scale of their decision in very different ways. For the already qualified, going on to higher education was merely the obvious next step; they held the possibility of higher education in the background, to be brought out when appropriate. Jenny, for example, was already qualified, as well as being married to a graduate. When her dissatisfaction with work grew she had no practical or imaginative difficulty in turning to higher education. 'I didn't really have to make that much of a positive effort to get a place, because I'd got the A levels . . . I always knew that it really only meant an application.'

For others who had a longer distance to travel, it was a project that needed more nurturing. 'From the age of the children being about three or four I'd done something in the evening – evening classes . . . an O level course in Economics'; 'I'd done the OU before coming here. I'd always done something' (Gwen).

But for a proportion of our sample higher education was more like another planet, unthought of and uncharted until some more or less chance occurrence. This group could look back to a period when a higher degree course was beyond imagination, the distance incalculable. They spoke of their own admission to it almost as a religious awakening – to a world that was known to be there but was thought to belong to others. Susan (at the subsequent interview teaching adults herself) described the distance she had to travel:

I didn't in my wildest dreams think that I could ever get a degree even at that stage, but I went back to evening classes to get some A levels – just to get some qualifications together and find out what I was made of . . . It was always a dream to go on to FE, even just an A level seemed a fantastic thing to do.

Geraldine also ended by teaching adults herself, and was similarly aware at the first interview of the distance she had just traversed:

At that time I didn't even realize that the poly only did HE courses. I got prospectuses in February – I found all these degree courses staring at me – I just laughed and thought there's no chance of that and put it away. I think that got me thinking – I dwelled on it for a couple of months but did nothing about it. Friends suggested an advisory interview – but I still thought it impossible and did nothing about it. I'd got a job starting when I'd finished my TOPs course and the last week I was on the course, I was walking to the bus station and I just wandered into the poly on the way and that was it.

Joanne also described the doubts and the distance, and her need for encouragement:

> I had a chance conversation with an acquaintance – a teacher – who said she didn't know why on earth I didn't go to college and get into teacher training. . . . That sowed the seed, but then I thought I haven't even got the A levels – the whole thing seemed enormous.

Drifting is a common image for school-leavers going on to higher education, and we offered it as a somewhat provocative description. In response, some acknowledged that the route had been easy or enjoyable. But many identified the element of struggle in their long haul through O and A levels. And some had wrestled with decisions about giving up jobs or rejecting alternative possibilites. Joy, for example, had 'got a good job'. Vera 'had to get three A levels first, which I'd done while the children were little – at night school'. Susan similarly 'had to really work hard – I had to sit for hours on my own – reading and writing essays'. Rae needed to settle her doubts and win confidence before committing herself:

> It . . . took a lot of thinking about, and before I thought I could even manage it – I kept thinking I'd be completely out of my depth so I really studied the matter – did a lot of reading in certain areas before I decided to do it.

But the image of drift was also understood in a rather different sense. Our respondents talked about the extent to which their pathway through the educational process and their route through to employment was planned.

There were some who had entered higher education with clear vocational objectives. In particular, and not surprisingly, those on teaching courses had a strong sense of planning. Some others felt that education had long been on their agenda and they knew exactly where it was taking them. Gwen said, 'It's always been there that I've wanted to do it' and Lindsay that, 'I was highly motivated and I definitely wanted to do it – it was well planned'.

But several respondents acknowledged an element of 'drift'. They referred to the tentativeness with which they had first approached the education system. Sally captured this experience most explicitly:

> I was so uncertain of myself. The big question was whether I could do it or not. It was a sort of well try it and see how it goes, without thinking of anything long term. Take it step by step.

Jean could imagine the start of the process, but did not commit herself to the career stage until she was on the course. 'I didn't enter it with the object of a career at the end . . . although I will go back to work.'

While respondents seem to be castigating themselves for this 'science of muddling through' the logic of their position is not hard to find. Many faced a great distance between themselves and higher education, they were uncertain of their academic abilities, and had many contingencies of family responsibilities to contend with. The process, then, was one of experiment, reassessment, opening up possibilities, rather than of building a plan around a clear goal.

In this respect our respondents were similar to other women in careers research. In her work on women primary school heads, Julia Evetts reviews her own results and those of other researchers:

> The careers of women teachers frequently lack a clearly defined end goal or purpose. From careers research (Hilsum and Start, 1974; Lyons, 1981) it seems that many men teachers have developed and followed a career route to, say, a headship position, moving posts, schools and even areas in order to acquire the necessary experience and achieve promotion steps and stages. Some women teachers will also do this, but more often they will have proceeded one step at a time (Grant, 1987, 1989). They see that they can cope with a teaching post and with their family and personal commitments. Then they begin to recognize the limitations of a new post in terms of what can and cannot be done. Then, and only then, do they begin to look around and contemplate taking the next step. There might be significant gender differences, therefore, in the attitudes of men and women primary teachers to career planning and development.
>
> (Evetts, 1990: 155)

Many of our respondents, therefore, entered the education world in a highly tentative manner. Miriam tried an O level course, with some hesitation: 'I thought about it for a year or so, then with [a friend's] persuasion for me to do an O level, I tried, and the result was so good, I couldn't believe it, it seemed so easy.' As described in Chapter 2, Heather used the same strategy, with similar results. 'I started off taking my Maths O level at night school because I was so chronic at school. And when I had proved to myself – the teacher was superb – and I passed it.'

Some took to the road without knowing where it was going, but with some hope that any qualification might help their employment prospects. Paula 'just thought initially an A level might give me a better chance when I wanted to get back to work' and Yvonne similarly 'started doing A levels . . . and that just gave me the confidence to think . . . well I can'. Lesley again describes the experimental approach and goes on to indicate the significance of the response from the education world:

> I don't think I considered going on to a university or polytechnic after I'd got this other A level. It was just . . . I'll get another A level and see where I go from there. But once into the system again . . . then you do start thinking towards other things.

For many these encounters resolved their lack of knowledge of the system, and their lack of confidence. A sense of purpose and determination grew after and out of these experiments:

> I went into the TOPs course more or less accidentally, and it was from then on I was continually fighting to do something to get out of the situation . . . It took a lot of courage actually . . . when you've been in the house for so long, you've got no confidence in yourself at all . . . from the very first day I went [to College] I suddenly realized I wasn't the only one . . . there were lots of mature students in exactly the same situation.
>
> (Kath)

The importance of their reception in the education world was mentioned by 17 respondents, though they were not specifically asked about it at this stage of the interview. The element of uncertainty or chance in these first encounters gave way to a sense of possibility once on the track, as the map was there to read. The existence of suitable courses, encouraging consultations with teaching staff, success on preliminary courses such as an O or A level – all were offered as important factors, as incentives to go on with the educational project. Such remarks often went with a sense of excitement about studying, or the possibility of success, or what education might have to offer in terms of career or personal identity. Thus many women felt that their recent experience of education was itself a motivating factor.

For Felicity the critical element was career encouragement. 'I went . . . to do some A levels. And the principal there edged me into teacher training, and said this is the sort of thing that you ought to be doing.' Joanne seems to have been excited about the educational experience itself:

> [The crash course] just made me keener. Once I knew I was on the way and made the commitment to give up my job, there was no looking back – that year goes down as one of the best years of my life – absolutely fantastic.

For some respondents the practical elements were strong. Education could be seen as an escape from a set of problems (how to earn enough money when a husband is on low pay), or a practical alternative to a job when children were young. For many there was a sense of education as a response to a crisis. Even those whose lives had gone smoothly could reach a blank wall after marriage and children. And others faced with mental illness or a broken marriage saw education as rescuing them from personal distress and poverty. There was a clarity about crises that needed resolving, about situations that needed changing. Others were preoccupied with the need for a change in themselves, for intellectual development and 'self-realization'. Some spoke of it as something for themselves – perhaps after years of putting children first. A small minority gave up careers and earnings in search of a liberal idea of education, turning to art history or archaeology as a complete contrast to a practical career.

Why education?

Many of our respondents could see little alternative to education as a route out of their various dilemmas. Some were giving up secure employment to take degrees; but many more felt trapped by inadequate qualifications and the need to combine earning an adequate income with parental responsibility. Nevertheless, higher education as a mature student is a minority activity; our respondents were often stepping out of line when they compared themselves with colleagues or housewives. The interviews contain some clues about why they turned to education rather than to other routes out of their dilemma, or simply putting up with difficulties.

Some made their own comparisons with siblings, husbands, friends and fellow students, suggesting, as we have in Chapter 2 that these may have been an important spur:

> I think I've always felt that I was only half educated . . . I rather joined the Communist Party on my husband's coat-tails so to speak, because his father had been in it . . . there are still things that I'm sorting out in my mind . . . the things I've been investigating this year are relevant to my critical interests.
>
> (Isabel)

They also picked up the theme of missed opportunities. Some students looked back on obstacles to better schooling, to interruptions to educational careers. Marilyn had been restricted by illness: 'I didn't start school until I was eight or nine because I had TB at the time, so I've always felt as though I was done out of my education. I felt I might have passed my 11 plus, but because of my illness they considered I wasn't well enough to sit it.'

Carol and Belinda recorded marriage and parenthood standing in the way of earlier educational experience:

> I did feel I suppose perhaps quite irrationally and unpleasantly that if I hadn't married I would probably have gone on to do many things in education and that I had forgone that.
>
> (Belinda)

> I'd always wanted to go back because I . . . I stopped because I was pregnant. I stopped half-way through the course.
>
> (Carol)

Rhona and Avril had missed earlier possibilities through economic constraints:

> I was always torn between doing nursing and teaching. In fact my parents were the ones who swayed me because . . . at the time they said they weren't going to pay for my education after 18.
>
> (Rhona)

I always knew I would come back to education. You see if I hadn't have had to earn my own living in the beginning . . .

(Avril)

Among all these comparisons with husbands and siblings, and stories of interrupted education lurk a number of characteristically female histories. For women of these ages, male comparators are likely to be more highly educated; marriage and parenthood would less easily have been seen as reasons for interrupting boys' educational careers; and, where there was a choice, economic support for girls in education may have been more readily sacrificed.

Conclusion

A strong theme in feminist writing about education has been that the education system turns girls towards domesticity (Chapter 1; Deem, 1978; David, 1980; Delamont, 1980; Finch, 1984). Some of our respondents' accounts suggest that schools had played this part in early life. But their perceptions of higher education at this point were entirely opposite. Now education was unambiguously the route away from domesticity. Whatever their experience of school, these women saw education as a route out of being a housewife and of the low-paid part-time jobs that go with that role. They saw it as a source of identity when being a housewife failed to perform that function, and when motherhood could no longer be the centre of their daily lives. And they saw it as a means of independence when the support of the family system failed. Respondents varied greatly in their attitudes to the family, and to bearing and bringing up small children; but they were almost unanimous in seeing education as a route away from the 'traditional' family pattern. Even where they saw education in terms of supporting their families, this led away from the most traditional family roles. Women's own perceptions are not the whole story, of course, and we shall discuss alternative ways of understanding these questions in the conclusion. But at the time of the first interviews they were not in doubt: education was going to increase their opportunity in the world of paid work. And while the mothers in the sample subscribed heavily to most traditional notions of maternal duty, they firmly believed that they could use education to escape from the housewife role, and the ill-paid, part-time jobs that now go with it.

Most also had faith in the possibility of career. A strong sense emerged of the limits of the position women found themselves in before education – whether of routine work they hoped to escape or of a career that they felt was no longer open to them. Economic pressures loomed large as well. Ambitions were not always precise, but nearly all respondents were opening up possibilities – looking to a future in which they would build a public career to complement or take the place of the private career of domesticity.

The destinations of these respondents – insofar as we have been able to trace them – suggest that their faith in education as a route to a new career was not entirely misplaced. This will be the subject of Chapter 6.

5

Educational Expectations

Education has one essentially dramaturgical purpose, that of allowing individuals to act out in a structured, publicly legitimated way, inner drives and longings. It is a presentation of the self to oneself and to others which, more than any other activity in life has precise, graded points of evaluation. The same is true of careers, or at least of public careers. It is not so much that society grants a higher status to career than to motherhood through any direct comparison but that the former is open to public evaluation. In the 'male' world of education and career, the inner sense of achievement only gains substance when it is expressed theatrically, to an audience that understands not only its public manifestation, but also its inner significance. In the 'female' world of home and motherhood, self-esteem has to rest upon ascribed rather than achieved worth, and hence often appears to be imposed from without. Where worth is felt, it lacks publicly certified validity; it has no theatre for its expression.

The family sociologist C.C. Harris once suggested that the late twentieth century parents have all the responsibility for the 'products' they produce, but legitimation of the age-old means – tradition, hierarchy, authority, control – was denied to them by what Martha Wolfenstein called 'fun morality'. As Harris observed, it is mothers who typically carry the burden of this dilemma: as parents they are denied criteria by which their task might be evaluated, but are nevertheless held responsible for the outcome (Wolfenstein, 1955; Harris, 1983: 24). In the late twentieth century, this poses particular problems for women. On the one hand is the growing formality of the division of labour and the still rapidly increasing process of credentialization; on the other is the marked erosion of the doctrine of the separate spheres with a consequent destabilization of the status of parenting and housewifery. At its most elaborate (say, in seventeenth-century puritan or late nineteenth-century bourgeois cultural formulations), the doctrine of the separate spheres could offer criteria for the evaluation of the female role with a moral and even theological certainty, but attempts to 'scientize' it or to incorporate it within the education system are, in practice, feeble. Dr Spock is a poor examiner compared with God or even with the strictures of working- and lower-middle-class respectability; in late twentieth-century schools childcare classes are strictly for the less able and domestic science is submerged beneath the waves of technology. Hopper and Osborn rather understate the matter when they comment that, 'It is not always clear to females in what terms their own education is justified' (Hopper and Osborn, 1975: 136).

The women in this study were educated at a time when the rhetoric of the separate spheres still had force and was, indeed, still acceptable in schools, but when the reality, for the majority who went to selective schools, was an environment geared to public examinations. Outside school, allowing for differences in class and background, gender was not problematic, though it was to become so. For most of them, and particularly for those who were first-generation public examinees, schooling presented contradictory messages and, on the whole, they backed away from identifying themselves with the full range of possibilities that the formal educational route offered. But as we have seen, when they reached the point of seriously contemplating the higher reaches of education, then it was clearly seen as the way forward, the way to shape or reshape a life seen as unsatisfactory. However, this confidence concealed a number of issues about education that remained problematic for our respondents and it is to these we turn in this chapter.

At the heart of Hopper and Osborn's theory is the discontinuity of role experience that they believed future mature students experienced. Amongst women this was felt especially by those of the younger generations in their study (Hopper and Osborn, 1975: 142). If we accept the argument that mass education increasingly incorporates marginal groups into its selective and credentialist process, this discontinuity becomes part of the experience of ever more women. Education systems may give some justification to the doctrine of separate spheres, but the whole weight of their credentialist purpose is thrown against such a belief. The issue for women, in this context, is one of deciding between conflicting sources of self-esteem; one (education and career) in which the drama is publicly acted, the other (domesticity) in which it is expressed internally, in a sense of internal integration, which presents only an image of contented passivity to the world – that madonna-like image of feminist opprobrium. Our respondents had reached a point where, for a variety of reasons, the second option was looking less attractive than the first, but it was not to be expected that this change would be unproblematic. Born into a culture where worth and esteem was expected primarily in worlds beyond the evaluative scope of education and work, they were now attempting to change the configurations of their lives. In seeking legitimacy through explicit, external evaluations of the self, they also experienced some difficulty with such a 'male', instrumental view of education.

In solving these problems we wondered if they might call to their aid a twentieth-century counter-cultural movement that has significance both for gender and class relations and that has found a particularly congenial home in those areas of higher education dominated by the arts and social sciences – the world most of our respondents entered. This is a movement best described by Bernice Martin when she explored, particularly in 1960s Britain, the opposition of the expressive to the instrumental and by Bernstein in his attempt to distinguish between the concept of the 'individual' and the concept of the 'person' (Bernstein, 1975; Martin, 1981). Bernstein's ideas in particular will be referred to again later in this chapter; here, drawing on the ideas of both Bernstein and Martin, we sketch the possible significance of this counter-culture to the experience of the women in this study.

Intense certification, and the strict evaluative accounting of human worth through education and work, is only one process of modern society that has particular relevance to women. This particular progeny of modernity has, in its turn, spawned a counter-cultural offspring, its own rebellious teenager. This is to be found in an intense narcissism that asserts that esteem lies only within the self, in the individual's sense of inner integration. Here the self constructs itself in terms of an almost mystical sense of inner coherence that may well defy the evaluations of the world, and indeed gains inspiration from such defiance. The counter-culture itself is constructed against an orthodoxy, opposing the secular, the evaluative, the 'macho', with concepts of the sacred, the expressive and the 'feminine' (see Cox and Pascall, 1994, for a fuller discussion). This counter-culture has, paradoxically it would appear, found a home within the educational world. The paradox is, however, more apparent than real, because between the structures that support the formality of a certified division of labour, there remains sufficient space and time for the cultivation of a narcissistic variant of the concept of a liberal education. Even more importantly, it is only formal education that can reconcile the opposition of these two cultures, by offering patronage, legitimacy and even certification to those who pursue narcissism. In Chapter 1, we noted that previous research indicates mixed and complex motivations amongst women mature students. We decided to explore the question of motivation and expectation in some depth, to examine the discrepancy between a 'sociological' view of education as instrumental, selective and status related and the somewhat romantic view of education as being an unmitigated benefit for a whole variety of more or less deprived groups including, of course, mature female students in higher education.

Needing education?

Examining the reasons why women return to the educational system, their rationales for doing so and their experiences of it, involves exploring their attempts to change their perceptions of themselves. Empirically this is a difficult exercise, since even in interviews, respondents tend to 'tidy up' the self-image they present, to show it as a state of being, rather than as a state of always becoming; to see themselves as encapsulated and unique wholes, rather than as playing half-learned roles to a half-comprehending audience, which, for most, is the reality of social interaction. Nevertheless, a series of direct questions about their expectations of renewed education were put that attempted to explore feelings about what they were experiencing, and, in particular, to explore possible tensions between the external and internal reconstruction of the self. Thus, the idea of education as a need was offered to them in contrast to education as a hobby (or even as akin to an expensive holiday), and they were asked about its significance to them in conferring status and authority, as well as being a route to self-fulfilment.

To ask a group of people if they need education is to invite a variety of answers according to how the word 'need' is interpreted. The need may indicate a lack of knowledge – 'I always feel so ignorant at times about general things' (Lesley); it may mean the lack of a specific qualification – 'I had got to have qualifications or whatever before I could teach' (Heather); or it may suggest a need to deal with something less tangible – 'it does fulfil an important part of my life' (Penelope). Such an ambiguous term does, however, allow what is most significant to the respondent to come to the surface.

Certainly, the question did prompt some responses in terms of needing education because it was instrumental to achieving specific work-related goals, including, of course, from those few who were on a course that included a professional teaching qualification. Michelle, for example, felt she only needed education, 'in terms of what I want to do with the rest of my life', and when asked a further question about what she expected to gain, the reply was, 'a specific job'. There were one or two others for whom the qualification was very important. Penelope, for example, wanted her degree because it gave access to jobs, and Isabel was aiming for something that would 'look good on job application forms'. Geraldine wanted to become 'a saleable commodity on the employment market' and Martha was characteristically direct when asked what she expected to gain: 'A better job. I've got to say that. I know it's not a popular view but it's definitely got a large part for me.'

For one or two, the process was not so straightforward. Cathy, for example, felt she was back where she had been at the age of 17. 'It's confirmed in me that I am an artist and not just a housewife who has a nice little hobby.' She was nevertheless left feeling uncertain about possible careers, and for Joanne it had originally been a means to an end, teaching, but had become instead a preparation for Christian service.

For the majority, including some of those already cited, the educational process was far from being exclusively work-related. Indeed, the unpopularity of having such an attitude, noted by Martha, was reflected in the somewhat defensive attitudes of several others, for example in Vera's reference to the 'instrumental thing', and Joan's to 'the diploma disease'.

Janet, for example, defended her sense of vocation in training as a teacher in special education. 'Money is part of it, but it's something that's going to be there for the next 30 years or so. It's a job that I wanted to do, a fulfilment, a great sense of satisfaction.'

Susan acknowledged that she wanted a career, but was concerned to qualify what this meant to her:

> It isn't so much a step up the social scale; that's nothing to do with it. I can see that people might think you are motivated towards a different life-style – but I want to be amongst people who think as I do, who can talk on the same level . . . feeling that I've got something valuable to say.

Val noted, not without a degree of distaste, something happening at her further education college:

> Our society is highly competitive, and getting more and more aggressive every day. As soon as I started doing A levels, I could feel the competition, the aggressiveness and the amount of industry that was being produced, that was coming out of this college . . . was quite phenomenal, and this, to me, was quite different from what I'd known at school.

Why should the educational route to career, money and enhanced life-style have been regarded so warily by these women, and why should they hedge about their desires in this direction with such qualifications? The answer, perhaps, lies in the view they took of the cultural value of education and, as we shall see, in their espousal of the counter-cultural force of a liberal education. This espousal, it would seem, was closely related to their gender.

Taking two questions together – whether they would describe themselves as needing education, and what they expected to gain from it – together with the various prompts, a discussion emerged that illuminated the way in which respondents perceived the experience upon which they had embarked. What was most striking was their awareness of the outward and inward looking ways of experiencing education, of the instrumental and narcissistic ways of approaching it. Take Dorcas for example:

> I suppose you could say it's an extravagance and a luxury for me to do this . . . I could be kept by [my husband], if I had to be. So I don't need it in that sense, but as a person I do – it's important to me . . . Psychologically it was very important for me . . . but needing it from an intellectual point of view – no.

One or two others also seemed to want to strip the 'need' to something almost elemental within themselves, to a belief that at the very core of themselves was something needing education:

> I used to say that I wanted to fulfil my potential – that was one of my stock phrases – and I feel that's what I'm doing. I'm just learning the

way how to do that. It isn't a hobby, or an escape from boredom – it is
me finding myself. I'm a totally different person than I was two years
ago.

(Susan)

It was merely to extend myself. I always knew that I'd got the ability to
get a degree. . . It was purely and simply for myself.

(Jenny)

It's fulfilled a basic need within myself. There were lots of questions
that I had never answered within myself. I started to ask myself
questions and it produced the definite need to get back to resolve
them.

(Marjorie)

Self education is a form of narcissism which is highly addictive and
several of these women recognized this. As Vera remarked succinctly, if
conventionally, 'education is part of life', and Rae happily concluded that,
'it's just gaining self-satisfaction and fulfilment'. Their scorn for the idea
that it was merely a hobby was almost complete:

It's too time consuming to be regarded as a hobby.

(Meryl)

I can find plenty of other hobbies that would not be so time consuming
as this, or so demanding.

(Lesley)

For three years, I mean I think one has to sustain a much more . . . a
deeper meaningfulness than simply a holiday.

(Paula)

It is perhaps significant that making the suggestion that education was
like a hobby caused some embarrassment to one of the interviewers, who
had, herself, been a mature student. But at least such outrageous
suggestions did prompt some thoughts about what education meant to
them, and these suggest not merely addiction, but an impetus that became
difficult to resist. Cathy expressed this most graphically. At the final session
of her adult teacher's certificate course, they were asked for comments.
Hers was simply, 'What now?' Similarly, Moira, after completing her A
levels found herself not satisfied, 'either to stand still or to move back'. In
their various ways, Sarah felt she had always been drawn to it, Rae felt she
was gripped by it and Jean concluded quite simply that, 'it's a compulsion'.

But these are not the conventional eternal students who are led to
education by background and the support of continuous, self-sustaining
success within the mainstream of the system. On the contrary their
motivation came from an understanding of education that could only exist
with such force in the latter half of the twentieth century. The concept of a
liberal education has been transmuted into a search for the self not only
through formal, public learning, but also through a private process, as

Kath expressed it, of 'structuring' the thoughts, of seeking that almost mystical depth of knowledge to which Paula and others referred. This understanding is of great significance to the cultural forms of late twentieth-century society. The formula that bears the secret of educational alchemy, that transforms the base self into a being, precious in its possession of hidden knowledge, has been passed in Western societies from priest to courtier, and from courtier to gentleman, even briefly in the mid-twentieth century to the aspiring sons of the respectable working class, to be taken up by women in their quest to change the patterns of their lives. Each transformation of an increasingly liberal and romantic education takes on the different characteristics necessary for the cultural force each successive group hopes to use.

The late twentieth-century women of this study use education to assert the primacy of the self and the possibility of its integrity against history, personal biography and the relative deprivation of their own education. Since gender is so significant a factor in that identity, women must try to lay claim to one mode of education and call it their own. Liberal education is thus made feminine, the alchemy of personal transformation becomes known only to women. It is often asserted that women are traditionally assumed to be more imaginative and creative, more interested in the arts and social sciences – indeed the women in this study frequently made that assertion. Clearly this belief has its roots in the doctrine of the separate spheres, but has been transformed by mass education into a belief in the particular relationship between women and a liberal education.

This quest for the holy grail of the existential self, however, requires secondary goals that are more explicit and tangible. There is, for example, the need for change:

> I felt I was vegetating. I felt this would open my mind a lot.
>
> > (Barbara)
>
> I felt I needed it at that time because I felt so stale.
>
> > (Yvonne)

And there is the achievement of change:

> I've changed more in these two terms, I think, than I did in the whole four years I spent nursing.
>
> > (Joan)
>
> I can tell by the conversations I have, especially with people I knew before I came on the course, how I've changed.
>
> > (Deirdre)
>
> The change has been fundamental.
>
> > (Kath)

Most tangible was the desire to test themselves and explore the limits of their ability. Sally put it most economically: 'Testing myself, testing my intellect.' What Paula wanted to know most of all was, 'if I was up to it', as did Felicity who, as the breadwinner, had all the external pressure necessary, but still had as a secondary aim 'to see if I could do it'. For some it was specifically to correct earlier failures. Marjorie, for example, had something to prove: 'that someone that had been written off by a grammar school, not openly, but in the subtle ways that they did write you off', could still achieve what had previously been denied or ignored. Marion was in a similar position, though her school had been a secondary modern: 'One thing I've proved to myself, that had I been given the chance earlier, I could have done far more. In fact I think I would have been a career girl.'

Martha had her brother in her sights rather than the school:

> I think I thought I was missing something. I used to think, well my brother's done really well for himself. What would have happened if I had managed to do O levels and gone through the process the way he did. So I think I wanted to know really if I was missing something.

From the testing and the trying again comes confidence, as it did for Janet, whose experience of further education 'did an enormous amount for me – not only giving me A levels, but the confidence to talk to people'. To which she added, 'I didn't realize how much I needed that.' Paula expected a boost to her confidence but also, 'a change . . . a hope to become more independent, a personality change'. These tangible expressions of the desire for change had a public dimension that might have been expected to produce an acceptance of the higher social status to which educational success might lead. However, what we found was a profound ambivalence about the relationship between status and educational achievement, and, indeed, an anxiety about the need to renegotiate the relationship between the public and the private aspects of their lives.

Status

In order to explore further what the educational experience meant to them, they were firstly confronted with the bald statement that education confers status and asked if this was important to them, and then asked if they expected to gain more authority as a result of their education. Ideas of self-fulfilment and of education being its own reward were only then introduced into the interview. For the interviewer to insist that education is primarily about status and authority is inevitably to challenge the view of education as being a process of self-exploration. The responses to questions about status, authority and self-fulfilment will be taken each in turn before attempting to discuss their expectations of education as a whole.

Many of the women's responses had, of course, been prefigured in answers to questions about needing education and about what they expected to gain from it. Nevertheless, the direct questions did provoke some very interesting and thoughtful replies and added a great deal to our understanding of their hopes, aspirations and fears. A small group identified status quite specifically with work and career prospects. Geraldine thought it would help in the employment market and Felicity made the point that many jobs, presumably of the kind she was interested in, specified graduate status as a requirement. Moira felt she was not concerned much with questions of status as a student, but recognized that she would be 'when it comes to employment'. Belinda rejected the link between education and status 'from a personal point of view', but recognized its value, 'from the point of view of getting on in one's job'. A couple contrasted their old status as nurses with what they anticipated as graduates, but whereas May felt she was definitely on the way up, Rhona felt the opposite, that in leaving nursing and entering teaching, she was on the way down. Alison, with two strings to her bow, as sociology graduate and qualified music teacher, felt the status belonged to the latter rather than to the former; for her the skill of the musician conferred status, the education of the sociologist changed the inner-self. The association of status and authority in particular with an almost technical sense of skill or knowledge was a recurring theme. With others there was a strong sense of catching up, of achieving a status that was due but had been allowed to slip away by default. Deirdre, one of the few who had actually tried to get to university and failed, felt that status was the reason she kept on 'getting qualifications and doing courses', and Helen, former nurse and from a well-educated family background, thought she would 'like to reach a status where everybody could see I was capable'. For Joan, who had taken A levels at school, it was the peer group from school that still influenced her and prompted the inevitable question: 'A lot of my friends from school had got a degree and why hadn't I got one?' Sarah was another with A levels and the beginnings of a career in the Civil Service before her family intervened who felt the lack of a degree. 'I was always thought a little bit inferior because I hadn't got one.'

Deirdre, Helen, Joan and Sarah made up one group who had really achieved quite a lot in terms of education or career, but who clearly felt that something was still missing, and that that something was a degree. They were counter-balanced by another similar group in terms of previous education and career, who flatly denied that a degree was going to make any difference. These included Rhona, who perhaps felt that she had made a mistake in deserting her nursing career, but also by Meryl, a qualified teacher, who felt she had more qualifications than most of her friends anyway and Lindsay, with A levels and a Diploma in Municipal Administration who said the same.

What this group of students, with some education-related status already to their credit, demonstrate is the relativity of status and the importance of where you have come from and where you hope to go to. But many of the students in this study simply did not have the sense of 'position' that allowed them to calculate the further benefits of an extra qualification. In educational and work terms they were in largely uncharted waters. For these women the question of status was clearly rather confusing. Surprise was not infrequently their reaction to the change in the way they were regarded:

It was a source of amazement to me that people suddenly saw me in a different light.

(Martha)

I don't think I realized that it did [confer status], strange as that may sound.

(Kath)

I don't know that I was actually conscious of it. I think now it is very important to me.

(Glenys)

Several acknowledged the significance to themselves of the effect of education upon status but with a certain amount of reluctance:

Well, yes, I cannot deny that.

(Paula)

I can't deny the fact that others who don't have it are impressed by it and that pleases me.

(Michelle)

I must confess it was [important], yes.

(Marjorie)

I suppose yes, if I'm honest.

(Marilyn)

To be absolutely honest, yes, it does play a part.

(Glenys)

A proper degree of natural modesty was no doubt part of the reason for this reaction, but occasionally there was more to it than that:

I know it confers status – and I'm really sad that it does.

(Kath)

I must admit that I'm loath to tell people I'm at college.

(Claire)

I don't think you should be sort of hallowed just because you happen to be going to a college or university or whatever.

(Heather)

Some denied the connection between status and education. Rae, for instance, flatly disagreed with the proposition that education conferred status and Yvonne simply didn't 'believe in any sort of hierarchy or status'. Whether it was the social phenomenon itself or the acceptance of its validity that they objected to is not clear, though it was probably the latter. Lesley tried to divorce herself from the taint of status seeking by claiming that 'relationships and friendships are much more important', and Belinda similarly tried to confine status to the world of work and denied its personal significance. Vera tried to deal with the problem slightly differently by acknowledging that having a degree would be 'quite ego-enhancing', and then adding, 'but only for myself'. Marjorie added a similar rider to her confession of its importance to her by saying that it was 'as much as anything to raise my own feelings and self-esteem really'.

Such comments go to the heart of the issue for many of these women. They were particularly concerned with the impact of education upon the self and the way that self was then presented to the world, not in a mechanistic sense of achieving a position, a role in life, to which status accrued by definition, but in terms of face to face interactions with others who are important and significant. As Joanne neatly encapsulated it, 'it alters your level of conversation', and it was in terms of linguistic interactions, above all, that the issue was considered. In such intimate encounters, to raise issues of status is to pollute the relationship with arbitrary, strictly irrelevant matters, so that, however much the thought of being a fully fledged member of an educational élite caused the heart to leap, it had to be kept a private joy.

Even Val, with her acceptance of an aggressive, competitive world, and a fierceness of expression that belied the anxious self-searching it sought to hide, knew her vision of the future involved intimate contact with people. She, too, was asked if status was important to her:

> Yes, it is, because I don't want to spend the rest of my life living with boring, stupid people. Somewhere there is the ideal group of people with whom I will instantaneously feel at home and fit in. But, I'm still looking. I haven't found them yet, but I know this is on the way to it.

Authority

Further definition of that 'somewhere' for our respondents came in their answers to being asked if they thought education would give them more authority in their relationships with other people. Here, especially, they had to confront their antipathy to the evaluative, certificate-orientated world they had entered.

Again it is useful to take Val as an illustration, since her belligerence makes her feelings absolutely clear. In her final year, she felt she had already gained in authority:

> Well, it's given me power and authority. Well, it gives you authority just in everyday situations that you have with people that you know fairly well, who try and talk a load of rubbish to you, who expect you to put up with it. And now I can see exactly what sort of games they're playing, even though they're not aware they're playing games. I can

tell them about it and cut them short, and I feel far more in control of my life now than I did.

Here was liberation of a kind, as there was in Deirdre's less abrasive feeling that it would make her 'a lot more assertive', and Joy, Paula and Gwen's expectations that it would give them a greater sense of equality. Penelope's wish was that it would 'redress the balance' and Dorcas similarly hoped that it would restore a sense of 'balance' to her feelings about herself. For Cathy there was the contrast with her previous life. 'Even as a student I have more status than as a wife or mother.'

Undertones of an uncertain female assertiveness seemed evident in several of these comments, as in some of their choices of alternative words. Other phrases that they chose in preference to authority included 'confidence' (Joanne, Helen, Janet, Juliet), 'a sense of personal achievement' (Glenys), 'a sense of personal worth' (Sally), and 'self-assurance' (Barbara). This was authority as seen by those who made no assumptions about it, whose perception of it was still, with one or two exceptions, frankly defensive, seeing it almost as a means of self-protection, better able to 'cope socially' as Jenny put it.

Another group identified a more technical aspect to authority, in the manipulation of knowledge. Moira identified this aspect very precisely. 'I expect to be able to put my arguments forward instead of feeling things and not being able to express them. That's more technique than anything else.' Similarly Vera felt she would gain 'intellectual authority', and that she would have 'knowledge to argue about things'. Claire was more concerned that it would raise in others an expectation that she knew 'a lot about everything', but May hoped to confine its effect to the handling of 'things', 'It would make me intellectually able to cope better in the way that I deal with things, but not in my personal relationships with people, I would hope.'

As before, so many of their remarks were overshadowed by this ambivalence about the effect that education would have upon them, particularly in the eyes of others. So often it seemed as if they wished to split the self in two. One part of them had an intense desire to change, to be different, more confident, more knowledgeable, more appreciated by people who matter, but there remained another part that wished to remain untouched by the experience, the same essential person, the unchanging self. Consider this response from Lesley when asked if education had given her more authority in her relationships with other people: 'I find it has, which is awful . . . Oh, it's horrible, because I cringe . . . I'm still the same person.'

Susan was similarly unhappy about the effect education had had in changing friendships:

> That grieves me really, that although you make new friends, you have to lose other people, because I'm still the same person. I don't do it to get more authority over other people – I'm doing it for myself.

Miriam regretted, but accepted the inevitable. 'You alter, don't you, with education. I think it probably will [give me more authority], but it's not something I wanted.'

Of the two who denied the relationship of education to status, Rae merely expressed her dislike of the notion that education confers authority, but Yvonne acknowledged that, 'It would if I wanted to use it.' Glenys, though preferring to think of what she had gained as 'a sense of personal achievement' rather than authority, felt, too, that it was open to abuse, 'In dealing with certain people, it holds a lot of sway which I abuse.'

Self-fulfilment

It was only when talking about self-fulfilment, that reservations, ambiguous feelings and defensiveness disappeared and the affirmations of the virtues of education were unconstrained. There was the occasional note of dissent, as from Felicity, who felt she got more fulfilment from her garden or her crocheting; and Martha related her enjoyment or lack of it to the degree of pleasure she got from specific courses. Vera was slightly sceptical about needing education for self-fulfilment, and Val was still searching, feeling that she had not been as aware of what was happening as she would have wished. For her, understanding, she felt, came only by travelling along a 'tormented route', but her commitment to her educational dream was clearly very strong.

Mostly, however, enthusiasm was unreserved and the comments mined a rich seam of belief in the personal value of education: in the satisfaction that came from meeting a challenge, proving that it was possible, overcoming the odds, and above all enjoying the struggle and the triumph. Michelle captured the thoughts of many of the others:

> It becomes a major ego trip if you feel that you can cope with the things that you are doing. The amazing sense of achievement must be . . . well
> . . . enormous, perhaps the biggest thing in your life.

Metaphors of growth, of extending and stretching, of expanding horizons, of not standing still, of deriving energy from the experience were all offered to explain both what was hoped for and what was experienced. Others chose slightly more sedate forms of expression, such as Helen who wished simply to become 'an obviously happier person', or Joan who was seeking 'peace of mind' and an end to the niggling regrets that had pursued her since she had previously abandoned education. Claire captured this best when asked what she thought self-fulfilment meant to her: 'I suppose it means deep down being happy, but not the sort of frothy happiness that comes and goes.'

There was also that sense of the inevitability of change, of the deeply penetrative nature of the educational experience. Comments ranged from Miriam's modest 'filling in the gaps of knowledge', Paula's feeling that 'it's nice to know things, generally, understand lots of things' to Isabel's 'sorting out ideas', Yvonne's growing ability to relate 'a lot more things together' and May's feeling of becoming, 'more critical, not in a negative way, but in an objective way, more analytical, maybe'. Then there was Dorcas's metaphor of 'enrichment', a satisfying exploration of one's thoughts, Moira's perception of a difference between 'words in black and white, and the meaning of them', and from Gwen the inevitable metaphor of depth again. The sense of change was most fully explained by Susan and Alison:

> You can't learn for its own sake . . . if you learn, it changes your attitude . . . you're bound to absorb it and adapt it.
>
> (Susan)

> I think it permeates everything. It's not just something that's collected and stuffed away. It permeates everything, the way you live and everything.
>
> (Alison)

Susan further described the process as one of 'finding out what's inside me', Lesley sought for that which was beyond being a wife and mother, that which made her 'feel a whole person' and Marjorie tried to capture a sense of heightened sensibility:

> Well, it means that it's filled this great big hole that was inside of me. It's given, it's given a lot, directly from the system of education, directly because I am now doing something I've always wanted to do. But it's given me a lot indirectly, because by feeling much more fulfilled, I see my family, my children, friends and everything, problems, in a completely different light. And they have a much more heightened meaning for me now.

Three of the women, feeling this growing sensibility, felt that it imposed a new responsibility on them. Susan, again, conscious of the changes education would require of her, felt the need to pass on her discoveries: 'First of all, I've got to find out, and then I've got to start trying to show other people there's more.' Joanne, too, felt the need to pass on what she had achieved. 'My idea of self-fulfilment is using what I've learned here, about myself, about life, for the benefit of somebody else.' For Kath, self-fulfilment was not an end in itself. In particular, she felt that she had acquired a particular responsibility to other women in positions similar to hers. 'It's more that I want to share it, and I want to know how to share it.' These three – Susan, Joanne and Kath – conveyed an almost explosive feeling of energy liberated by the understanding of some great secret. For them education had unleashed this energy and they felt they had to share it with others.

Cultural forms and educational aspirations

Most of the women in this study, to some degree or other would seem to have espoused a culture based upon what Bernstein has called personalized organic solidarity (Bernstein, 1975: 125). He argues that the increasing complexity of the divisions of labour in advanced societies produced not one but two forms of organic solidarity. The individualized form is that identified by Durkheim; the personalized form that is generated by the growth of middle class occupations concerned primarily with cultural and symbolic control as opposed to economic control, and with processes of reproduction as opposed to those of production. The growth of these agencies of symbolic control led the new middle classes to develop cultural forms that challenged, not class relations as such, but the mode of their reproduction. The cultural manifestations of these two forms of solidarity have their own 'distinctive and conflicting ideologies . . . forms of socialization and symbolic reality' (Bernstein, 1975: 125). In his discussion of the differing approaches to socialization that these opposing modes of reproduction entail, Bernstein describes their differences as follows:

> Whereas the concept of the individual leads to specific, unambiguous role identities and relatively inflexible role performances, the concept of the person leads to ambiguous personal identity and flexible role performances.

In common parlance it is the difference between a civilized, properly socialized individual, and being oneself and doing one's own thing. What Bernstein appears to be suggesting is that the concept of the person arises as a counter-cultural movement attempting to transform the concept of individualism by reintegrating the inner self with its civilized presentation. The self-control that produces the inflexible and restricted role identities is no longer necessary. However, the encapsulated self becomes more intense and more defiant in its attitude towards the society beyond the self. Whether this, as Bernstein would have us believe, is specifically a product of the rise in the late twentieth century of the new middle classes, or whether its twentieth-century manifestation is but one transformation of a cultural dualism that has always been part of the process of civilization is a moot point. Nevertheless, the idea of a cultural opposition centred on differing conceptions of the self and upon the way it dramatizes itself to the world, offers an explanation that can relate apparently ephemeral cultural and ideological expressions to the changing economic and social structures of contemporary society. Bernstein has the particular virtue, in this context, of having worked out his propositions in relation to education and to the way in which education relates to the social rules of cultural transmission.

It is at least plausible, theoretically, to suggest that middle-class women seeking to change the patterns of their lives, but structurally still confined to activities and occupations that are overwhelmingly concerned with reproduction rather than production, will espouse the personalized as opposed to the individualized form of organic solidarity. Further, should they seek to challenge and oppose an orthodoxy, either because they are women opposing a male orthodoxy, or because they come from working-class origins and seek to challenge middle-class assumptions, then the orthodoxy they must seek to oppose, or interrupt in Bernstein's terminology, is that of individualized organic solidarity.

It would be easy to describe the way the women in this study talked about education in ideological terms, to see them as exponents of a fairly straightforward belief in equality of opportunity and in education as a universal right. It would be similarly convenient to put a political gloss upon their reservations about, and reinterpretations of, the connections between education, status and power: about three-quarters of them left school in those optimistic years between the mid-1950s and the late 1960s and returned to education when the women's movement was beginning to surface. There is, undoubtedly, a 'progressiveness' about their views on education and gender that fits in well with such an interpretation. What such an explanation fails to explain, however, is the wider and deeper cultural base into which such ideologies are embedded, and the evident ambiguities and discomforts that ideologies so often generate when they are confronted by the lived experience of particular individuals. What it especially fails to explain is the extent to which these women were products of the clash between opposing cultural forms of the kind outlined by Bernstein.

As girls, many of them learned the unambiguous and inflexible role identities appropriate to marriage and motherhood, but their relative success within the education system gave them glimpses of other possibilities, and their ambiguous attitude to work hints at a fleeting recognition of the possibility of greater role flexibility and a broader, but more ambiguous sense of their personal identity: not only as a wife and mother, but also as a career person. To the extent that it is merely work that is involved, this might not disturb the equilibrium too much, but work that is associated with high levels of education is an altogether different proposition. The old class, says Bernstein, holds that variety must be restricted so that cultural reproduction may take place: the new class seeks variety in order to challenge and oppose the structures of the old class.

The sense of anti-structure (see Martin, 1981:49) was quite strong amongst the women in this study, perhaps mostly in relation to their experience of marriage, but also in their deliberate espousal of 'progressive' educational values. In particular, it was evident that the new self that was to rise from the educational baptism, thoroughly cleansed of the old inadequacies and inner confusions was not merely to play another, different, pre-determined, unambiguous and inflexible role in life, but was to change in a fundamental way the relationship between the self and the world and, indeed, to act upon the world in new, positive and active ways. The rules of living were to be changed in a most significant way.

But there are deep contradictions involved in the pursuit of personalized organic solidarity and our respondents experienced some of the personal conflicts that these entail. A cultural form that has at its heart the concept of the person as unique, integrated and self-contained is always going to present difficulties to people whose position in the configurations of social life is changing. Add to that a cultural form in which there is an expectation that the inner core of the self will manifest itself to the world in its total integrity, but at the same time will remain free of stereotypical roles, and the inevitable result is anxiety in anyone seeking to change themselves and change the perception that the world has of them.

Was it because of this that quite a number of these women desired, at one and the same time, to change and yet to remain 'the same person'? It was of particular significance, perhaps, that though there was an intense desire to change inside, to be different, more whole, more secure and confident, there was nevertheless a great reluctance to express this in terms of new, socially recognizable roles. The imagination seemed reluctant to project the new self into concrete – unambiguous and inflexible – role performances that would proclaim them a new 'individual'. Instead what they sought to convey was a desire to be a new 'person', confident in the freedom of the self from the old constraining roles.

Status and authority are concepts that belong firmly to the world of individualized organic solidarity, to forms of cultural reproduction where social positioning is clear and where criteria for evaluation are explicit and unambiguous. Education in modern societies has a major role in delineating both the positioning and the evaluative criteria. It is therefore scarcely surprising that those women who espoused so strongly the cult of the person, should express reservations about the effect that their own education was having upon their claims to status and authority. To admit, unreservedly, the importance of education to their future status in the eyes of the world, would be to admit the inevitability of the pollution of their desire, not to adopt a new set of roles, but simply to be a new person in the world.

Bernstein describes the contradictory position of the new middle class, by describing the variance between the theories that they hold dear and their objective class location. The former denies the validity of explicit rules of cultural reproduction, whilst maintenance of the latter is dependent upon precisely such explicit evaluation and certification. As aspirants to new middle-class status – for where else could they go – these women not only become victims of the contradictory nature of its position, but also find the problem compounded by gender and by their own histories.

Their own biographies, indicating as they so clearly did discontinuous and disrupted histories, suggested lives where the process of cultural reproduction, or what Abrams called the process of becoming, took them along untrodden paths (Abrams, 1982: 267). But the choices that they took led them inexorably to seek support and comfort in a set of cultural propositions that are highly ambiguous when faced with an uncomprehending world.

As the women themselves acknowledged, it was their own histories that directed nearly all of them to the arts and social sciences. Some saw this concretely in terms of the lack of science in their previous education, a few in terms of some more mystical, feminine inclination. Whatever the cause, the majority found themselves studying subjects where, to use Bernstein again, the academic structure was one where the classifications and framing of knowledge and its organization were at their weakest (Bernstein, 1975: 100). Equally, the cult of the person was probably at its strongest and as students they inhabited academic worlds (the humanities, the 'soft' social sciences, education) that appeared to value the person above and beyond the specific roles that they played. Such worlds are far from being exclusively feminine, and there are other ways for women to challenge constraints upon their lives, but the oppositional nature of the cultural forms suggested by Bernstein's personalised organic solidarity provides the kind of cultural base that promises support in reshaping the inner self. How successfully the women negotiated their way through the rest of their lives, will depend, as did so much of their previous lives, upon the contingencies they encounter in terms of work and personal relationships, the strength of their commitment to the counter-cultural spirit of personalized organic solidarity, and their capacity to reconcile its defiant mysticism with a rationalistic, evaluative world. Some of the possible answers to these questions can be glimpsed in the next two chapters when we turn to the results of the second interviews.

6

Reassessing Education: Careers?

Returning to interview our respondents in 1992, we focused on questions of career and of identity, the subjects, respectively, of Chapters 6 and 7. Our questions on careers were intended to give a picture of current occupations, of working lives, and of career mobility. We also wanted to make some assessment of the impact of education and other possible factors on the development of careers.

Work experience

Current occupations

Nothing in the literature on women's careers led us to expect respondents to be over-represented at the top of employment hierarchies. Higher levels of education for women are associated with higher levels of participation in the labour force, especially in full-time work (OPCS, 1991: 53); and a degree may well insulate women against the worst labour market experiences, with which several were only too familiar at first interview. Comparison with unqualified women would show our graduates at a great advantage; but comparison with similarly qualified men tells a different story. Recent evidence is that the pay gap for women in higher levels is actually greater than that for manual workers (IRS/EOC, 1991: 3). In particular women mature students in a Northern Irish study were outraged about interview and promotion experience (Morgan, 1981). And Brown and Webb found that 'Neither men nor women [mature graduates] appear to have the same range of opportunities as their younger counterparts, but age and gender combine to ensure that older women experience the greatest degree of constraint and exclusion' (Brown and Webb, 1993).

Respondents at first interview were often caught in a web of family duty, combined with inadequate educational qualifications, or with qualifications and experience they could no longer use. The educational deficit was the one element they could actively change. But the rest would not just disappear. Many of our respondents experienced changes in family demands over the study period, but they were not free in the sense that most 21- or 22-year-olds are free – free from family duty, to put their own career first, to move to better employment. An economic recession hindered employment prospects, and some respondents found age telling against them as well as gender. These may not be circumstances to nurture personal ambition.

Our respondents themselves gave us greater expectations. They were unusual individuals, choosing to be mature students when this was relatively uncommon and Access little known. They demonstrated personal qualities of determination and dedication that must have read well in many an academic reference.

In practice the pattern of employment in the second interviews was quite different from that in the first. Our first sample fell into two, with roughly half in office or shop work or similar, and the other half in management or professions, with most of these in nursing. There were now a clear majority in professions, with none in nursing: six school teachers (including one retired), one FE and one HE lecturer; two librarians, both with professional qualifications; four social workers, one research assistant, and a GCHQ translator. Of the six in administrative jobs, half had clearly managerial responsibilities, including one in social services, another in the urban programme, and a health service contracts manager. The other three were classified as doing more routine administrative work, though one of these had considerable responsibilities as a secretary in an industrial company. Some respondents were climbing hierarchies, especially in social services departments, but also in schools. Finally, one respondent had turned from a successful career in a social services department to set up her own business. The pattern of employment at second interview was much more clearly rooted in the professions and higher administrative occupations. It was also overwhelmingly public sector employment (20 out of 23) and full time (apart from one reluctant and one willing part-timer).

Working lives

> Every time I go to work, on Monday morning most people hate going to work, but I love it, I really do. Obviously you get bad days, boring days and stressful days and things go wrong, but I never feel that I want to throw it away.
>
> (Susan)

Not all accounts of working life were as enthusiastic as this. But changes between interviews in responses about the nature of work were more dramatic than changes in occupational categories just described. At first interview a high proportion experienced oppressive boredom from routine work far below their capacities, and this, in particular, had changed. The few left in routine work told the same story now, 'A total experience of boredom and frustration' (Moira). Some, like Geraldine, moved through unsuitable jobs (in this case accounting) wondering 'What did I go through all that for?', but moved on to better things (now lecturing). 'Now, definitely not boredom, I never suffer boredom in my job' (Geraldine). Some found aspects of the work tedious. 'A lot of paper work you do, administration, is a bit monotonous' (Janet), but not the essential core, in this case teaching. 'I don't get bored with the children.' But the resounding response showed people interested and absorbed by their work. 'I took the job of team leader and I felt from then, that role and since then has been very challenging and stimulating' (Kath). The positive experience of such occupations was particularly noticed by respondents such as Susan and Kath who had moved across the boundary from routine work.

More respondents acknowledged frustration. Sarah had difficulty finding appropriate work: 'at the time looking for work, after you've done all that studying and what have you achieved at the time, nothing at all, so at the time it was very frustrating.' Dorcas, who was excluded from post-graduate training in psychology, described herself as wanting 'to work with adults, and very frustrated that I couldn't do that'. Val, now a secretary in an industrial company, reported, 'I've never had a boring day here. It's just that I sometimes look at myself and think I am only this, this is not really good enough.'

Nearly all worked in public sector occupations, and their accounts reflected the widespread discontent of public sector employees in the early 1990s. Geraldine, for example, resented the changes in higher education. 'I think it's difficult for me being a student in the department, and remembering what it was like to be taught in the department when I was there, as opposed to how it is now.' Janet enjoyed teaching but had similar feelings about education. 'The SATs, that's a whole issue by itself, that is incredibly frustrating' and 'education is in a pretty poor state in some areas'.

Some respondents expressed reservations about career structures. Jean enjoyed her work as a librarian, but felt it was given a 'low priority within the administrative department at the place I am working . . . there's no career structure whatsoever'. Gwen acknowledged the frustration of career aspirations that could not be reconciled with her wish to practise social work.

Women's work is often seen in terms of personal relationships. Moira expressed this most clearly in these interviews. 'I tend to go to work to be with the people, rather than [for] the job itself.' For this reason we asked about companionship at work in both sets of interviews. In previous interviews there was some dissatisfaction with the nature of relationships at work – especially among office workers. This time, there were some women who were working in relative isolation: 'it's a one-man band basically, you work on your own' (Jean) or 'I tend to remain on the periphery and I think that's probably why I'm quite happy to do two jobs, because it means in a way that you don't get too involved in either one of them as far as colleagues go' (Penelope). But most accounts were of work environments that were socially rewarding as well as personally satisfying:

> It's very good, I have a very good social life with the people at work. They have been very supportive, I've had a recent bereavement and the people at work have been very good about it; they are very good to work with, it's a nice place to be.

> (Gwen)

Economic aspects

Dorcas, trapped reluctantly in part-time work, reacted brusquely to our question about recent employment and economic security. 'No, it certainly hasn't given me any security, very little.' Penelope felt that security lay in her marriage rather than in her employment; and there were some whose economic situation was not much changed. But some had been through severe economic straits, especially as single parents, and had now achieved an economic security rarely available to women outside professional or managerial occupations. Helen needed 'a worthwhile career' and 'a reasonable pension', which she achieved as an established civil servant. Geraldine and Susan were single parents with young children:

> I'm just about getting there now, just about. It's about five years since I graduated. I spent years paying off the overdraft and things, so just about.

> (Geraldine)

> It's beginning to just pay benefits now . . . yes the economic side has had a lot of attraction for me really, especially going through university as a single parent, struggling, because it was a struggle.

> (Susan)

Others saw security in terms of contributing to a marriage. For example Vera supported her husband while he established himself in business, and others had found finances perilous in marriages where they had no or part-time earnings:

> Not that I didn't need to earn in that sense, but it wasn't a priority, it was a need within myself. Circumstances have changed such that it is fortunate that I did go into higher education, because I have become the main breadwinner.

> (Jean)

I suppose I was looking for two things, to some extent it was financial security I was looking for, which we hadn't had in the early years of our marriage; that was one aspect of it.

(Lindsay)

I never imagined in my wildest dreams that we would live in a house like this.

(Michelle)

These responses suggest the unexpected. Few of our respondents had admitted that economic ambitions dominated their quest for education; there was little to lead them, as women, to expect to achieve financial security through employment, and this may have led them to make economic ambition a low priority. But a high proportion had moved from more or less acute financial constraint to a degree of security.

A number of our respondents had never been dependent on husbands or partners; others had come through a patchwork of relationships and relationship breakdowns; yet others had maintained stable relationships. Independence had different meanings in these different contexts. Val, for example, stressed personal independence: 'I have always had financial independence. I have never been dependant upon a husband or boyfriend. But I have always been and felt totally independent.' Geraldine had been through single parenthood and living on a grant. 'I've just gone from a grant to earning my own salary now, but I think I do, I'm told, I give the impression that I am terribly independent.' Heather and Claire on the other hand talked about independence in terms of being able to contribute to the family:

It's helped us to move house. . . and I feel much better being able to earn money, that I can contribute.

(Heather)

Before there was always a guilty feeling that I was spending someone else's money, I would have to give an account at the end of the day, not that my husband was ever like that, he never asked me . . . it's certainly nice now being able to contribute, to earn something in my own right.

(Claire)

Several respondents examined the relationship between financial independence and personal independence. For those still with young families, the constraints of full-time work meant restrictions on personal choice. Lindsay remarked that she had 'financial independence, but in many ways I have a lot less freedom than when I was at home', and Gwen likewise found, 'It's given me security, it's given me a certain amount of independence, though the constraints of having a family mean you are not independent.' But others saw financial independence as giving rise to personal independence. So Susan remarked that 'it's beginning to just pay benefits now, and I've found that it makes me very, very independent', which seems to make the same connection as Val's remark above, 'I have always been and felt totally independent'. Moira – whose work situation was unchanged – made a different kind of connection, this time between education and being able to work independently:

> I feel that they are employing a brain as well as a person. That thought never occurred to me before, I did a job in a certain way because that's the way it had been done, but now I feel I have the right to ask questions, the right to say to a supervisor 'this is what I expect of you' rather than it being the other way round, and the right to say 'what do you expect of me' rather than wait to be told.

Overall, and with some exceptions, the picture was of women who had achieved a measure of economic security and independence, which some associated with a greater sense of personal independence. Like other women in their occupations, most were not at or near the top of hierarchies, and their income probably lagged behind that of comparable men. But a good proportion were more economically secure than they had ever expected.

Mobility

The opening section compared the employment patterns of our two samples. Shifting employment patterns may be looked at another way, in terms of individual mobility, which was how respondents experienced it. Their lives should be studied against a background of women's experiences more widely. What we know of women's careers is that they are often characterized by downward mobility, with full-time 'careered' employment giving way to part-time, relatively low-paid work combined with unpaid family responsibility (Martin and Roberts, 1984; Brannen and Moss, 1991). This pattern is changing, as each new cohort counts the cost of 'giving up work to have children', but continues to dominate, and certainly did so for the age groups represented in our sample. Indeed, many of our respondents had already suffered some downward mobility before taking their degrees.

All but three of the second sample had spent most of the interim period in full-time employment, and 16 had experienced a measure of upward mobility comparing pre- and post-degree occupations. Twelve of these had crossed a crucial divide in women's employment between routine clerical or shop work – non-manual but with very limited career prospects – and some form of professional or managerial work. Five were at a similar level to their earlier employment; one had slipped down, and one had climbed a career ladder and was now stepping out into her own business. This picture contrasts sharply with that of women's employment in general. Two-thirds could be described as upwardly mobile in their employment, and two-thirds of these had moved from jobs with few prospects into careered occupations. A minority were on a sharply upward path, moving into higher management positions in teaching, social services or the health service.

Most of our sample had achieved occupational mobility, moved into professional or managerial work and showed a very different picture from their pre-graduate experience. In these respects their experience contrasted with the pattern of women in general. However, for some their degree appears to have made no difference, and some had lost ground. Some aspects of the occupational pattern were unglamorous; there was a new form of segregation into the public sector, which is found in other studies (Brown and Webb, 1993); few career paths were meteoric, and while most of our sample appeared economically more comfortable than before, they were not in the highest-paid positions.

Not all our sample were upwardly mobile in career terms, and their careers had so far taken few into the upper reaches of professional and managerial structures. But the personal significance of their moves was reflected in a number of comments expressing surprise, even astonishment. Belinda 'didn't see myself becoming as senior as I am now', Geraldine 'would never have believed that I would get into this kind of career, not ever, not even when I graduated'. Those who had stepped over from routine work into managerial or professional occupations felt that they had moved into another world:

> If someone had said 'well that's what you will be doing' I wouldn't have embarked on it, I just needed that extra confidence at each stage.
>
> (Michelle)

> I can't quite take it in sometimes that I have got a job where I am given a good degree of responsibility and freedom to do it my own way.
>
> (Susan)

> I've been managing budgets, for example, and involved in policy-making, I would never have envisaged myself being in that situation.
>
> (Kath)

Another question encouraged respondents to measure the distance travelled, and to assess the impact of the educational experience on it. 'Can you imagine where you might have been without higher education?' was greeted with some bafflement. Some respondents felt that there was no distance to be measured. 'I would have been exactly where I am now' (Isabel). Others found it hard to imagine, 'No I can't, not really. Very dissatisfied I think' (Michelle). But some found graphic ways to describe the future that had not happened:

> I think I would have been doing something largely unskilled. Possibly very hard work physically, not a nice picture at all.
>
> (Val)

I was a shop assistant and I guess maybe I could have moved into some kind of supervisory role, with experience, but that would be all.

(Kath)

I dread to think. I would probably be working at – I don't know – my sister's working on petrol pumps. We have the same family background, she went to grammar school. My other sister's working in an office. I would have been the same . . . So all I can do is think about how it would have been if I hadn't done it and I can see that I have benefited tremendously, physically, mentally, emotionally, in every way really.

(Susan)

Explaining

Theoretical approaches to understanding the position of women at work are understandably preoccupied with disadvantage. Briefly, the explanations for women's disadvantage are sought in human capital – relative lack of educational advantages; discrimination – practices in the work environment and trade unions; the Industrial Reserve Army – the creation of a pool of part-time low-paid workers who can be readily brought into and out of the labour market as capitalist development demands; and the relationship between paid and unpaid work, where women are put at a disadvantage in paid labour by the demands of domestic labour. These theories are of restricted usefulness here. Our story is not one of failure, on the whole. Also, we are limited to seeing careers through the eyes of individuals, and this kind of evidence is more pertinent to some kinds of theory than to others. Nevertheless, such a large body of literature about women's work gives us clues about what to look for, and our data may shed some light on the theories.

We asked our respondents to reflect on the relationships between their education and work experience (human capital) and on the way they were treated at work (discrimination). They told us about their family lives, though not this time in response to direct questioning. These categories should help us to understand the relative success or failure of these women as a group, and perhaps to shed some light on what differentiates the more successful in our sample from the less. The reserve army notion may be more useful in explaining the marginal labour market positions from which about half our sample came, than in appreciating how they had escaped their fate or where they were now.

Education and career

We asked our respondents whether their education had fitted them for the job market and for the occupations they had eventually got. Had it failed them in any way? What other significant influences were there to take into account?

Appropriateness of qualifications on the job market was a factor mentioned by some respondents. It would not be surprising if women so inhibited about the idea of developing a career should choose courses less than carefully in this respect. It is widely acknowledged that women in general do not take those courses that give the best opportunities in the job market; these women in particular may have been restricted in their choice of degree, with science qualifications not necessarily available to them. Most of our respondents had been students of arts or social science subjects, and some of these felt that the degree in itself was not enough, or did not give them a clear sense of direction:

> Now perhaps I do feel that I could have done a more useful degree, careerwise.
>
> (Val)

> I think with hindsight now I chose economic and social history because that was an interest, but I realize now that I would have been better going into a vocational sort of subject, like sociology . . . because that seems to have more career prospects for mature, married women.
>
> (Claire)

Felicity and Meryl were already qualified teachers, and the rather specialized degree that Meryl took (in genetics) may have made her position worse. Geraldine, too, wondered whether she had been misdirected into a career in accounting. 'I think I was encouraged along the wrong paths', but was ultimately able to change direction into higher education, so 'whether or not that ended up as a good thing or a bad thing . . . it's difficult to judge'.

But more of our respondents felt that the degree had helped them into a much more favourable position in the job market. For Susan it took time and further qualifications. She followed her arts degree with a one-year Masters in Information Technology. Even then it was some time before the opportunities opened up. 'I was beginning to think that degrees themselves were meaningless, although I had enjoyed doing it, and had got a lot out of it, but on the job market you were either over-qualified or under-qualified or hadn't had the experience.' But once she found her way into further education she had exactly the right combination of skills:

> It was a real shortage area . . . people were desperately needed, not so much with a science background, but with an arts background, particularly communication skills . . . I knew that I needed to make myself employable and that is what higher education did.

Gwen, Sarah and Kath had all used a social science degree followed by a Certificate of Qualification in Social Work to establish a social services career. Gwen remarked that 'it fitted me very well for employment. It narrowed the field, well it should do after five years, but it's definitely fitted me for employment. I don't think I would have any difficulty in getting a job. It's served its purpose in that way.' Like Susan, Sarah felt that the sense of direction and appropriate employment were a long time coming:

> It was very disappointing to come out and find you had to wait such a long time to find what you want. But I feel now that qualifications do give you a certain status when you are looking for jobs.

Finally, Marjorie discussed her degree experience in terms of the skills and confidence that would enable her to set up in business. Her rather too meteoric rise in the social services was followed by health problems and the need for another new beginning:

> Because I've done that degree it's enabling me to feel that I had got ability to do something, so when it came to a crisis point last year, I knew I could pick up further training. I knew that I would enjoy that because I just love learning . . . The degree – which teaches so many other things apart from academic knowledge – means that I can go into something new and know that I can take it on board and have a really good go at it. It also enables me to have skills to put things over to people, teaching skill, counselling skills, because of that discipline of pulling together and analysing and then being able to use it.

So Marjorie felt her education had fitted her for employment 'in a far more wide ranging way than I would ever have appreciated'.

Our respondents will have suffered more than younger students from the accreditation boom, which left earlier qualifications (e.g. teaching certificates and nursing qualifications) inadequate, and turned degrees into a stepping stone rather than a bridge into professional or managerial employment. Age and constraining circumstances may have meant more than average frustration with the process of becoming qualified, and sometimes a failure to reach the other side. In some cases – though not all – the unspecific nature of arts and social science qualifications was found to be a disadvantage. But with these reservations, the most general feeling from our respondents was that their degrees had done exactly what was needed in career terms, and often much more than was expected.

By the time of the second interviews our respondents were exceptionally well qualified. All had completed their degrees, and several had gone on to further training. Postgraduate professional qualifications in teaching and social work appeared to be effective keys to satisfying employment. As noted above, Gwen, Sarah and Kath had postgraduate qualifications in social work, two of them MAs. Among the teachers, Penelope did a conversion course in maths and then a Post Graduate Certificate of Education (PGCE); Susan a Masters degree in information technology and an education certificate; Michelle a PGCE, and an RSA (Royal Society of Arts) in drama in education. To raise her status in librarianship Jean did a one-year MA in library and information studies and followed this with acceptance as a chartered member of the Library Association. Helen considered following her language degree with an interpreters' course and felt that 'it would have been better' if she had; now established at Government Communications Headquarters (GCHQ) and thinking about promotion, she has applied at work for training in Japanese – 'which is one of my languages which I have totally neglected . . . It would seem to be quite an asset to have at work because it's a rare language.' Many had done practical training, from Val's shorthand and typing to a collection of work-related courses.

The need for postgraduate training was emphasized by Susan, who felt her Bachelor of Arts and Humanities was an education, but 'it didn't fit me for any job. I had to go on and train afterwards.' Val felt that she should have done some kind of postgraduate training to further her career, but had other, family, priorities at the time. It may be that 'women's' careers are particularly demanding in this respect, and it is certainly the case that Val and Dorcas, who did not manage the further training they would have liked, paid a high price.

Respondents also discussed fitness for employment in terms of capacity to do the job. They fell into rather different categories in respect of the vocational element in their degrees. For some teaching courses the degree was a purely vocational enterprise; for some students in arts and social science the degree itself might be everything, and any occupational advancement a bonus. The first group naturally stressed the accreditation side of their degree experience, and had some tendency to scepticism regarding the connection between education and their practical experience of work. For example, Felicity thought the only skill her degree gave was computing experience she could use in the classroom; and Heather remarked, 'I don't feel that a lot of what we did at college was totally relevant but I also knew that, it's like your driving test, you've got to go along and prove yourself in a lot of different areas in order to get this licence to teach.'

The non-vocational students may have had lower expectations of any vocational uses of education and were rather more positive about any utility they could find. Some respondents emphasized the use they could make of their degree in terms of performing a job better, rather than of the qualification needed for appointment. Isabel, for example, was already a qualified librarian. 'I think having a degree is the icing on the cake as far as my career prospects are concerned, because . . . I had a professional qualification before and quite a lot of experience . . . it was the content and the course itself, rather than a piece of paper . . . what I actually learnt on the course I have very often drawn on.' And despite Joy's first thought that 'there's nothing vocational attached to a degree in sociology', she went on to talk about how research methods and urban studies had helped her work on the Urban Programme. Moira felt her degree may have got in the way of promotion in the Civil Service, but that it had helped in the work, 'from the management point of view they have got a better deal out of me. I find the more demanding the job the better I can cope with it.'

Marjorie's account of the development of abilities of wide ranging use in employment is most widely echoed in discussions of confidence. While it was not always clear whether confidence grew as a result of the degree or of subsequent employment, there was a widespread feeling that this was a fundamental change. Vera argued that 'being at home does undermine your confidence' and this points to a particular meaning of confidence for our respondents: they appear to be talking about the ability to deal with the public world, and especially the world of paid work. Janet remarks that higher education 'had the effect that I did become more confident, which does change everything else to a certain extent'; and Dorcas 'always used to imagine that other people were a lot cleverer than I was . . . I'm prepared to challenge people now'.

Susan – whose eloquence before the tape-recorder was unparalleled, even in these interviews – claimed, 'I hadn't got the confidence to see myself in any high position . . . ten years ago I wouldn't have dared speak into a tape-recorder.'

Vera's closing remark that she felt 'very much still the same sort of person just with more confidence really' gives some measure of the importance of confidence for our respondents. This concern is echoed in studies of women returning to training courses, discussed in Rees (1992).

A prominent theme of the first interviews was the need for a new career. Some respondents lacked qualifications for a career of any kind, and felt a great need to involve themselves in work that was more absorbing and rewarding than their previous experience. Others had qualifications, but found family work and the paid work for which they were qualified to be mutually exclusive. Others found that any period out of employment had set them behind. Returning to this subject, we found the same kind of interpretations. Claire had trained as a radiographer: 'there have been tremendous advances in the treatment of cancer in the years between . . . there was no way I could actually go back to that'. 'I worked for the Inland Revenue . . . you can't return to any position that you had before, you have to start from the bottom' (Michelle). 'After having my children I wouldn't have been able to get back into the bank at the level I was at' (Gwen). 'I wanted something that would offer something interesting, and my husband wanted me to have something that I was going to enjoy doing so that he didn't feel guilty that he had given up work and was living off me' (Vera). Neither librarian felt this kind of need for change, and both returned to library work, in one case moving up from assistant to professional capacity. Belinda felt that she had used her degree to shift emphasis rather than to start again. 'I don't think that graduation was a gateway to something greater and better . . . because I already had a very senior post when I was studying . . . I got interested in a particular aspect of the work I was doing and decided to take a turn in my career and progress it in that way. So it gave me the wherewithal to be able to do that, in fact to do it better.' Neither Moira nor Meryl had found the new career that they had hoped for. Moira made the best of her experience and hoped that it would help her progress in the end. 'It hasn't given me anything in career terms, but what it has given me is a different attitude to day-to-day existence in my career, whether ultimately that will pay off I don't know.' Penelope put her response in context. 'I wanted a new career, I also just wanted a degree.'

Three or four of our respondents were clearly disappointed with the impact of education on their working lives. The sharpest sense of disappointment was expressed by Dorcas, unable to get postgraduate training for the professional practice in psychology she had in mind. 'I think disappointing really is one word to describe it. In fact it's been a bit of an anti-climax really.' Dorcas was nevertheless doing research work that required her degree experience, albeit in a part-time and assistant capacity. Moira had been unable to use her degree to escape from the Civil Service or get promotion within it. Meryl, despite two degrees, was somewhat stranded in office work and felt that education had 'not really helped, though it's something that I haven't regretted and going back in time I would still do the same thing'. Val, better employed than before her degree, but now in secretarial work, was quick to point out that it was not the 'fault of education'; having no outside support she had made a deliberate decision to put her family first.

There were also respondents such as Isabel, who had a career as a librarian and for whom education met other needs; and some for whom education had been clearly useful, but might have been expected to have taken them further. For example, Jean had made the move into professional work as a librarian but found her pay and promotion prospects not much better than before. Marjorie might have liked to 'continue the academic path' but was unable to travel to the research work that she was offered; her 'career' had not been smooth, but nevertheless she felt she was using the skills she had developed, and the 'degree will be the one thing that I will never, ever regret doing'. Felicity had made two 'returns' to education; the first period of teacher training had given her access to work which she found rewarding; the second return, to achieve degree status, seemed no fortification against age and gender discrimination.

But most of our respondents were satisfied that their educational experience had fulfilled the role they intended as far as career was concerned. The sense of satisfaction was well expressed by Jean. 'I have a professional qualification, I have a good job. I have job satisfaction.' Lindsay was unusual in that she 'knew exactly what I wanted . . . and everything I did on that course was with the end product in mind'. Gwen expressed a more common uncertainty, a need for qualifications combined with a less definite sense of where they would take her. 'I don't think when I came here I wanted to be a social worker. I think that developed while I was here; but it broadened my mind; it gave me lots of ideas; it did what I wanted it to do.'

Overall, the mobility we have measured shows that our respondents did achieve the new possibilities they sought, and in many ways went beyond their expectations. The accounts of working lives also show a pattern of much greater satisfaction with employment than we found earlier. Experience had played some part in these improvements, but our respondents were inclined to see higher education as playing a crucial role, in accreditation, in developing skills and in developing the confidence to deal with the public world after periods of confinement to private life.

The level of qualification at the second interviews was unexpectedly high. There is no lack of human capital in our respondents. In many cases degrees had been supplemented by further degrees, professional qualifications and other training. Overall, their qualifications seemed unduly high for the level of employment they had achieved.

The family

The second interviews asked in a rather simple-minded and limited way about the impact of higher education on career, without specific questions on the family. But the complexity of our respondents' lives prevented simple answers. When family duty jostled with career obligations respondents were unable to describe a career in one sphere without reference to the other. As before they were preoccupied with questions about the appropriate balance between public and private duties, and with how to manage the tensions that arose; explaining themselves involved histories of public and private lives.

Most had chosen some kind of mixture of private and public duty that involved giving neither ultimate significance. Some had solved most immediate dilemmas by waiting until the children were old enough to care for themselves, though this would not have been without career costs. Many described ways in which career had been limited or compromised in order to accommodate other family members. Isabel worked part time in order to give herself space between family and work obligations. Sarah spent a few months at home with a four-year-old and some of the following period in a job share. Lindsay referred to family illness hindering the extra work required of a teacher in an administrative grade. Val felt her daughter's needs did not allow her to invest everything in her own career. Dorcas chose not to pursue a particular career line so as not to put pressure on her marriage.

A number felt that family commitments restricted their mobility, and thus their range of choice. 'Because of my situation I had to stay in this area' (Meryl); 'I had the problem of mobility because I needed to stay within this region, because at that time I still had two sons who were at school' (Jean).

Not all comments about the impact of family duty on work were negative. Three partnerships had taken decisions that made the woman's career more important. These involved the woman taking on greater financial responsibility, while the man set up in business, took a cut in income for the sake of congenial work, or early retirement. The family also appeared as a stimulus, 'bringing up my own children made me open my eyes to teaching'

(Lindsay), and, as described below, women often saw the skills developed as a parent as a useful resource in paid work.

However, the overriding impression from these interviews was that domestic duty was a restraint on unbridled ambition and the single-minded pursuit of career, though its impact varied greatly according to the age of children and availability of other support. The logic of the position adopted by many of our respondents was rather painfully illustrated by Marjorie, whose more single-minded pursuit of career resulted in crisis, and a conviction that this idea of career needed rethinking:

> Because it's seen as the best way to assert yourself as a woman or to show that you are as good as men . . . to actually get out there and get the career and prove yourself and get into the senior management posts, well I'm not actually sure whether women ought to be shouting more about 'well hang on a minute, maybe we just don't want that way of doing it, there are other ways of doing it'.

Discrimination and sponsorship or positive and negative discrimination?

Hoping to disentangle education from other possible sources of career development, we asked respondents to consider whether any opportunities or influences from outside education were relevant to their career advancement. A few mentioned the support of friends and relatives, but in terms of influence on themselves, rather than on anyone more powerful. 'I had a couple of friends who were also doing the same thing . . . so I suppose it was a bit of influence from them . . . It was my parents' expectations as well. Although I was married with two children, they still had aspirations' (Joy). Susan and Val interpreted the question negatively to describe discrimination and lack of support. Susan had met more or less overt discrimination at a job interview, and Val talked of the constraints of her family situation: 'If I had more living relatives or more money, or more assistance from other people, I could have perhaps looked after my daughter and gone off and started a career. But I really couldn't depend on anyone but myself.'

The nearest we came to an account of procedures favouring women with children was in Sarah's account of social work selection, 'possibly the fact that I had brought up a family – at the interview – I feel it counted for something in social work'. But the benefit was strictly limited to selection: 'It didn't count for anything financially.'

In general our respondents had more to say about hindrances than good fortune. No one mentioned any kind of sponsorship, or any happy chance except that for which they had directly worked and applied.

Among the negative sources of discrimination, age was a factor. Moira and Dorcas, two of our more disappointed respondents, reported:

There's a time bomb in that now I'm 53 so therefore I'm being perceived as someone who doesn't want a career ... if there's an opportunity for promotion and I want it, I have to spell it out, and it was in fact my boss who advised me to do this.

(Moira)

I did psychology and I really wanted to be a clinical psychologist and I got a good enough degree to do that, but the thing was I discovered I was too old to get into the course.

(Dorcas)

Kath described a very active career but felt age was a hindrance. 'Once I'd got qualifications the opportunities opened up, not vastly, because of all the difficulties in terms of getting work once you are older, I think.'

Very few respondents described sex discrimination, but Moira, stranded in her old Civil Service job, was an exception:

I pushed to go on the transfer of part course which would put me into more interesting, demanding work; and there is an examination title course, which again I'm having to push to get myself on it, whereas a man who joined the department on the same day that I did, he's told that he is top of the list for it. We were on the other course together ... and we did the best on the course, I did the best and he did the next best, I had to push harder to reach the same stage all the time. But again I will have to write to management asking again why I am not on the course. But I shouldn't have to. I feel I have to be more abrasive than I want to be.

The contrast with other respondents reflects the earlier interviews, where those in routine work described particular and direct discrimination, while those in professional occupations might be aware of structural features – 'headmasters are men' – but did not feel personally ill-treated. Respondents' experiences of private sector occupations seem to have been largely unhappy. Geraldine's brief experiment with accounting, followed by a more successful move into higher education, is one example; and Val's secretarial position in an industrial firm is another.

Respondents' structural analyses were more overt and extended in the second interviews. Librarians, social workers, teachers, lecturers and managers were all working in hierarchical organizations, where the pattern of recruitment to higher positions is very clear. They were now very well qualified, all with degrees and some with further training. Some had made steps up the ladder. Some had been exposed to studies that made them particularly conscious of gender discrimination and organizational cultures. From this emerged a considerable preoccupation with the hierarchy and their place within it. Thus Geraldine commented on her minority status, 'it's a very, very male-dominated department ... I was the fifth female to be employed which is not very good really out of 35', and Marjorie on contrasting roles, 'the department seems to have women carers and not many top women managers'. Kath and Jean described hierarchical structures:

> In most social services departments, probably all in the UK, from team leader level upwards it's very male dominated . . . In our senior management group there's one woman and six men.
>
> (Kath)

> Most of the library assistants are female, and it is also a profession that is predominantly female, but all the top posts go to the men, and this is borne out in the surveys by the Library Association.
>
> (Jean)

There was little accusation of discrimination in personal terms, but few were quite so positive as Helen, working as a translator at the Government Communications Headquarters (GCHQ):

> There's no gender discrimination in my job, not at any level. It's like a technical job. People look for your linguistic ability first, and if that's there that's it.
>
> (Helen)

Kath, despite her lucid account of management culture and gender discrimination in social services departments, felt fortunate in her personal situation, partly because the social services as an organization 'does value the more feminine style of management', and partly because of her immediate superiors:

> I think I'm actually quite lucky in the organization that I work for, in that there are actually two men who are immediately above me as seniors, that's the manager and assistant director. They are both aware of these kind of issues and actually seem to value the skills and abilities that I have. So I feel in that immediate network of people I am actually quite lucky.

Susan commented positively on the need for women in her area 'once I'd gone into it the red carpet was laid out for me' and on her authority's equal opportunities policies.

As in the earlier interviews some respondents said that women's work brought no direct experience of discrimination: 'I work in a very, very female-orientated situation . . . I am with women who are like myself . . . So being a woman has made no difference at all' (Janet). 'I have only been in one school and my headteacher has been very supportive; apart from him we have a complete female staff and all the management team at the school are female. In that way no problems' (Lindsay).

But Claire found that 'there's a fairly paternalistic attitude at work'. Jean had to distance herself from clerical work, but 'that has been overcome, you establish yourself . . . you provide a service that they realize they need, and they realize then the extent of the professionalism that is involved'.

Felicity described going back to teach:

When I went back to school, I went to the head and said 'What are my prospects now I have got this degree?' and he said, 'None here, I won't advance you any further.' He said he would block any move I made to leave.

Felicity seemed to tell this story without rancour and without direct accusation of sex discrimination. But the story appeared in a discussion of being a woman at work, and she evidenced some sense of entitlement to promotion. So this was the nearest we came to an accusation of personal sex discrimination in a professional context.

The Irish teachers interviewed by Valerie Morgan were vociferous about their treatment in interviews and promotions. 'The great majority of them did in fact succeed in getting jobs quite quickly. Their anger and indignation arose particularly with reference to interviews for jobs, and to a lesser extent, with reference to promotion' (Morgan, 1981: 46) and 'almost all wished to talk about promotion and almost all accepted, albeit with some anger, that they were very unlikely to be promoted' (ibid.: 50). There are a number of possible explanations for the difference between Morgan's respondents and our own. One is in differences of time and place. Northern Ireland in the late 1970s and early 1980s may have been more overtly discriminatory against mature women with families seeking paid employment than would an East Midlands area some years later. But the nature of the respondents' qualifications may also have made a difference, with the professional teaching qualification establishing more sense of a claim to employment status than our respondents' mixture of qualifications, including arts and social science degrees.

An intriguing feature of our interviews, especially the second, was our respondents' recognition of structural features of discrimination in their occupations, alongside their relative lack of felt experience. In the light of the structures – which are well known – it seems unlikely that the discrimination felt and described was all that took place. It is more likely that in these employment contexts discriminatory practices are covert and/or indirect – for example, favouring qualities and experience more frequently found among men. It also seems likely that our respondents did not see discrimination because they made so few claims for themselves. Few appeared to make any claim to career improvement stemming from their own qualities and qualifications; this applied to the most 'successful' in career terms, as to the least. They showed more surprise at how far they had come than resentment at having gone no further.

Career strategies

Finally, we may be able to understand women's position at work by examining career identities and career strategies. Our data suit this approach, so much of what we know being through respondents' versions of events. We would not want to convey that the strategies adopted were independent of occupational structures: if women's career strategies did not always seem designed for the fastest progress, it would be too crude to put the blame at their door. Their decisions must be understood within the context of structures that are clearly unfavourable to women's advancement, and cultural expectations about unpaid work that affect most women's choices about paid work. This section attempts to make sense of women's career strategies, looking at three aspects of women's careers: working practices, career planning and career ambition. Each may be significant to the ability of women to climb career ladders.

Working practices

We asked whether being a woman made a difference to the way respondents handled work. Talking about being a woman at work produced a wide range of replies. Geraldine, a single parent with young children, talked of the problems of balancing work and family:

> I like to think that I don't fall back on that, as the excuse for not doing things . . . I think I do probably feel different about the job because I'm female, . . . because I have to spend so much time doing other things.

Lindsay clearly devoted mental energy to the same problem. 'I think being a woman affects my attitude to work very much . . . I think I am constantly balancing home and work – even though my children are teenagers and one of them is in her twenties.'

But others stressed the more positive aspects as they saw them. There was an emphasis on organizing abilities developed as a parent: 'I am very well organized and efficient' (Dorcas); 'you have to pay attention to two or three different things at a time and plan your day . . . I think being a woman and having home responsibilities enabled me to do that' (Susan).

Relationship capacities were widely seen as another strength that could be brought to bear in social work, teaching and management. Three teachers made this point. 'I am very much more aware of my students and how they are feeling and I think I can put them more at ease' (Penelope); 'Women wanted a woman teacher, women seem to relate to a woman teacher'(Susan); 'I got closer to some of the children and they felt confident coming to me if they were in trouble' (Felicity).

Two managers made claims to a distinctive and valued style:

> As far as being a woman is concerned in doing the job that I do, I think that helps me enormously. My relationship with colleagues – I think a lot of it is to do with personality – they accept a lot of things that I ask them to do, and the way that I ask them to do them.
>
> (Michelle)

My preferred style is a participative style of management and actually sharing with people and helping people bring on their strengths, which tends not to be the style used by men.

(Kath)

Belinda was clear that she was not going to treat being a woman as a disadvantage, or to see discrimination round every corner. 'I have always tried not to blame anything I have not achieved on the fact that I am a woman. I have always thought that I am as good as any man.' Penelope speculated about her care not to be seen lacking in any way, describing a specially conscientious approach to her work:

I have never met any sort of prejudice. Whether or not that's because I have always been on top, always been very well prepared, always been obliging in what I have been prepared to do over and above normal lessons, which has ameliorated any feelings they may have had, I don't know.

Overall, the impression was of women who valued the qualities they had to offer at work, which they saw as deriving from experience in the family, and from being stretched between work and family. While they were obviously not impartial judges of their own working qualities, their claims should be seen against a background of the interviews as a whole, in which there is a considerable amount of self-blame.

Career planning

In earlier interviews respondents were often conscious of their lack of career planning. They share this characteristic with women in other studies of women's employment. Brannen and Moss even say that 'the defining feature of these careers . . . was the absence of a sense of "career", either in terms of time or of long term rewards' (Brannen and Moss, 1991: 49), and compare their findings with those of Julia Evetts on primary school headmistresses (Evetts, 1988). One explanation they give is that 'this short-term employment perspective was because women were highly oriented to the lives of their children and focused long-term planning on them rather than employment careers' (Brannen and Moss, 1991: 253).

In the context of the uncertainties of their lives – about marriage and family – and the obligations and lack of qualifications, their self criticism seemed overdone; and their step at a time procedure – adding a qualification here or there, opening up possibilities – seemed more logical than they gave themselves credit for. Some uncertainties had been resolved by the second interviews. In particular, families were probably complete; most women were in long-term relationships, or established on their own; and most had a clear career direction, often with a professional qualification.

But questions about the extent to which education had fulfilled their plans, taken them beyond their plans or failed them altogether tapped into this area again. For some respondents, mainly teachers, the degree decision was a career decision, after which they lived in relative certainty. For others, a degree opened up possibilities but did not establish a direction; as the section on education showed, this could leave uncomfortable uncertainty after graduation. Not surprisingly, therefore, respondents differed widely in their discussion of this area. However, there was a frequently expressed sense that they did not plan to be where they were now, and could not have done so, as Claire says 'I didn't really have any intentions'. For Michelle it was a matter of establishing confidence:

> I had to take it in stages, first of all I thought I would be an infant teacher, I could cope with five-year-olds, then I thought maybe I could do seven to eleven, and then to actually end up teaching 16-year-olds within the first week of my employment . . . I just needed that extra confidence at each stage.

Janet, having established herself in teaching, could now put promotion on the agenda. 'You know you are coping with your job and you can go for a bit more now.'

The absence of an idea of forward planning and its replacement with opening up possibilities still seemed common among our respondents, if not as much as before. As a way of accommodating uncertainty, lack of experience in the public world, and heavy commitments in the private world, this strategy was rational, but it may well not have been the best route to top positions.

Career ambition

Studies of women in careers have found women expressing reservations about career ambition. 'In the construction of their employment careers many women themselves imposed limits on their ambitions' (Brannen and Moss, 1991: 68). Morgan's study of mature students suggests that career ambition may not be so straightforward for female students as for male. Morgan found that, 'Interviews with mature men graduates produced more candid less embarrassed statements about their deeply felt need to improve their position in life, usually with reference to salary and status. These more worldly issues were rarely mentioned by women' (Morgan, 1981: 36). To some extent, our own sample reflected this earlier evidence. We had no men for comparison, but our women had also been reserved about career ambition in earlier interviews, preferring to put reasons of personal development first in their accounts of their move to higher education. Economic issues in the earlier interviews were about economic survival rather than riches, and here again, despite their considerable success, there is a degree of ambiguity about the idea of career. For Sarah, her degree was about 'a personal sense of achievement, academic achievement, I really didn't go into it thinking I was going to get a fantastic job out of it'. Geraldine 'never had any big ambitions about what I wanted to do. It was just a case of surviving really'. Both Susan and Felicity balanced the rewards of advancement against its costs:

> A friend of mine offered me a chance to go and work with her at the poly but it seemed to me that I would need to make some hard thinking decisions about the importance of career in my life really . . . I might be happier with the kind of college student I've got now.
>
> (Susan)

> If it had been offered I would have gone on to be head of department, if it had been offered, I wouldn't have gone out of my way to look for it or been bitchy or backbiting . . . I wouldn't descend to it. You have got be very hard, not too bothered about keeping friends or making people dislike you . . .
>
> (Felicity)

Helen appeared to accept career in an uncomplicated way, neatly expressing the classic idea of career as life's focus: 'I wanted to do it as a basis of a new life, a new career and a new life.' But there was among our respondents a sense that they were not eager to embrace all aspects of the idea of career. For many, career seemed to be an important part of life but not its central force.

A number of interpretations may be put on this finding. One is that it is a matter of acceptable expression; as Claire said: 'Obviously just because you don't express an intention doesn't mean that buried within you there isn't a desire to have a fulfilling life, and obviously, I didn't want to be just a housewife once my children had grown up, so there is a stimulus there to do something so you are not just a housewife.' Naked ambition is not a socially acceptable characteristic for women, and they may learn to express themselves in other terms.

Another possibility is that women may tailor their ambitions to their expectations. Some are already very conscious of being behind in the race for high status jobs. Vera said, 'I'm obviously not going to be a director of social services.' She was referring to what she saw as the handicap of a late start, but she might well be referring to gender too; women directors of social services are not thick on the ground. Women have reason to feel that career structures are against them; numerous studies point to women having few places at the top of hierarchies (Hansard Society, 1990). Career structures built around a traditional male pattern of a 40-year span in full time employment put most women at a disadvantage; our graduates in particular – with age against them – may have felt they were starting several laps behind.

Another possible source of ambiguity is the nature of career demands in relation to unpaid work in families. The traditional male career pattern depends on a measure of service, with women 'Married to the Job' playing supporting roles (Finch, 1983). So Susan remarks that 'men doing the same job as I am doing, they go home and they've got cleaning ladies and various people to cook the meals etc. Other female members of staff have got the same experience, when we go home we take on another role of mother, housewife.' Val makes a similar point: 'Men are allowed the luxury of only having to have singular field of vision, so I think all women everywhere, to my knowledge, they have to work harder, they have to try harder. They don't go home and find that their wife has the tea on the table, or all their shirts and blouses are ironed.' Marjorie – in the light of painful experience – entered a discussion of the merits of women attempting to run successful careers and families at the same time:

> I think a lot of thought now should be going into whether women should be expected to follow the same path as men. I think there are a lot of issues about what actually men should be doing.

While these patterns may be changing, women still expect and are expected to support other family members rather than receiving support themselves. In the section above on family duty, we found our respondents' experience to be one of meshing public and private lives rather than single-minded dedication to one or other. Our respondents' idea of ambition may well be more complex than simply ladder climbing.

Finally, the nature of the work involved in a career post drew comment. Several respondents described their preference for front-line jobs in teaching or social work over managerial activities. Thus Heather 'never had any ambitions to be a headmistress. I'd much prefer to be in there doing something', and Lindsay, after trying an administrative post:

> found in the end an awful lot of the things I was doing weren't satisfying. Being with the children – that kind of interpersonal thing – and seeing their progress and their development, that's very import-ant to me. But the other things that were involved in the career structure . . . in the end could be done by somebody else, it wasn't something that perhaps needed me.

Gwen remarked of social work 'either you go into management or you stay at that level, there's no career structure if you want to stay working with people, you have to go into management to get on, and that's not what I want.' The suggestion seems to be not that she would not be interested in a career, but that she was not interested in career development as currently defined. Gwen described this more graphically when she described her 'frustration because of the way things are, that I can't be, that I feel left baggage shall we say at having to be a social worker on the ground rather than working up.'

This discussion should not be understood as implying that careers are not important to women. Our respondents wanted satisfying and re-warding work – work they could see as socially useful. A high proportion concurred with the idea that they wanted a career rather than a job, and many had gone to considerable lengths to get one through higher education. 'I didn't want to get stuck in a job with no progression or nothing to aim for and work that left me uninspired and bored' (Janet). They enjoyed the economic security that work as graduates now largely brought them. Those whose career aspirations were disappointed had put great effort into job applications, and those who had prospered in the job market showed no lack of dedication to their employment. But it does appear that there is a degree of ambiguity around the acceptance and pursuit of career as it is currently defined. Not only is the classic career pattern one that fits a male working life; but also the environment within which women work sends daily messages about the unlikelihood of career success. While some women may respond to this with rebellion, not all appear ready to put their lives on this particular line.

It could be argued that the current environment gives women an opportunity to choose an approach to career that is largely denied to men. In a period of such intense change in relation to women's careers, there are no socially correct answers. This could be seen as liberating them from any particular version of career choice. Such liberty is not without problems: our respondents showed some anxiety about this subject, and there are no answers without costs. Putting the family first is likely to lead to part-time work, less mobility, and less satisfying and rewarding work. Going all out for both may lead – as it did with one of our respondents – to overwork and collapse. Putting career above everything costs women the family in a way that it does not cost men. We had no examples of such a strategy in this sample. All our respondents had balanced family and career demands in one way or other, though in some cases major family duties were now left behind. This choice, usually to include family and attenuated career, was easy to understand within the context of social practices at work and in the family, and it led a high proportion of our sample to a great measure of satisfaction, if not to the top of their careers.

A more critical way of looking at where women are placed in career and family would be to argue that the prevalence of an idea of career and patterns of career development that are inconsistent with most women's lives is a form of discrimination, to which some measure of opting out is the most acceptable answer.

The evidence of our respondents was that a number of obstacles existed to making a career at all, and to making a career life's object. For some, these were overwhelming, and respondents had not been able to make use of their degree in conventional career terms. For most, obstacles represented delay, or less preoccupation with career advancement, but did not prevent employment that was both economically and personally rewarding.

7
Reassessing Education:
A New Person?

In Chapter 5, when discussing our respondents' reactions to the experience of being a student in higher education, we felt that there had been a heightened awareness of the self, a search for a new identity, or for the 'real' self that the contingencies of life had suppressed. This search had led to a good deal of anxiety and, indeed, scepticism about the propriety of education conferring status and authority. This sociological 'orthodoxy' about the function of education was opposed by our students through their espousal of what we termed a counter-cultural view of education as sacred rather than secular, as directed to the inner self rather than to the outside world, and, perhaps, as distinctly 'feminine' rather than 'masculine'. We suggested, however, that though this counter-cultural defence against a secular, rational, 'macho' world might be relatively effective within the safe haven of higher education, it would present considerable difficulties later. In the second interview we asked them to reflect again upon questions of status, authority and self-fulfilment, offering back to them some of their remarks from the first interview. We also asked them whether they thought the changes that they had undergone had proved to be merely transitory or genuinely transforming. What follows is a general discussion of the ways in which their perceptions seemed to have changed since the heady days of living the life of a mature student.

Person or individual?

In the second interview, the sense of anxiety about identity seemed less acute; there was a sense of distance and of perspective. Reflecting upon their time as students, a few of the respondents used words like 'odd', 'weird' or 'mad' to describe how they thought people must have regarded them then. But there was also less concern about this. Jean, for example, suggested that she was not 'much bothered how people perceived me' and Lindsay claimed that she was 'fairly thick-skinned'. They were now some distance from the heady, if anxious, experience of student life. Students could be described, in terms of their stereotypes: 'walking around in old clothes', 'chatting and lounging about'. This is not to say that the experience had lost its significance, but in Bernstein's terms, which we discussed in Chapter 5, the concept of the 'individual' had perhaps reasserted itself over the concept of the 'person' (Bernstein, 1975). Being a student was now to be viewed as playing a role, not the search for the Holy Grail that it had once appeared to be. Sometimes, however, it had taken them to heights they had never reached before or since. Take Isabel for instance:

> It was very satisfying to write essays and read deeply and have the time to read and write. I found that very satisfying and occasionally I read some of the essays I wrote then and it seems like another person did those. I can't believe I actually had all that inside me, and it's probably still there somewhere, you know, so it was a very satisfying four years. But I got it out of my system. I don't feel that I want to go any further academically. That seemed to satisfy me, those four years. It does change you I think . . . not the biggest thing in your life . . . it seems a long while ago now.

Emotion recollected in tranquillity produced a sense of perspective, but they also found a residue of something permanent, 'deep down' as Michelle put it. Nevertheless, the sense of a clearly defined role that came with professional and responsible work seemed more important during the second interview. Susan described it like this:

> I feel I am doing something worth while, so I feel quite privileged to be doing it and that gives me a great deal of satisfaction. Yes, part of it is about self-fulfilment, you're finding out that you are not just a mum, a sister or a daughter or a wife or just a drinking friend, but also that you've got different facets to your personality . . . I look around me at work, that a woman with growing children who goes back into an interesting career, isn't subject to the same sort of depressive illnesses, lack of self-esteem that a women who stayed at home feels. The adrenaline's going, you're busy, you're occupied, you're happy, you're fulfilling a role in life.

The playing of roles had perhaps become more acceptable. Claire, for example, acknowledged that as a student she had been in search of the 'individual' self, separate from the 'dependent' self as wife or mother, but now that was achieved:

> I just know I'm an individual now, I have a life apart from my family and husband, I'm worthy in my own eyes. Whether other people still perceive that no longer matters to me because I know that I'm making a very worthwhile contribution at work, so it no longer matters in one sense.

A role that is publicly acknowledged, has no need of the concept of the person. Indeed, Claire, discussing the concept of authority, went one stage further in stressing the separate worlds she could now inhabit. Clearly in her job she exercised considerable responsibility and had to work with many different authorities and agencies, but this was to be kept separate from the world of her friends centred on the Church. Perhaps because she was a woman, perhaps because of the nature of the Church, the authority was not transferable, and her Church friends, she suspected, had little idea of the extent of her responsibilities at work.

Another factor that stressed role rather than the integrated person was the demand that work made upon the organization of personal and family life. Claire, again, was typical of several in stressing the imperative of effective time-management in running job and home together. Lindsay too found her life 'far more mapped out because there are so many things that I have got to do, whereas as a housewife I could do as I liked in the daytime to some extent'.

Val had taken the business of playing roles one stage further:

> I have always believed that whatever stage you are at in your life you sometimes go into an area where you are a person who is in a special category – like you're a new mother, or you're newly bereaved, or you've just had a nervous breakdown, or you are a hospital patient, or you are a student. And as soon as I entered the world of being a student, I sussed it out immediately that here was something different . . . Then I looked around for another category that I could jump into, that had the same sort of benefits. I'm playing now a woman whose daughter has grown up and if I want to go out and buy lots of clothes, or go to the theatre, I can do exactly as I want to.

Claire's interpretation was more sober, but just as interesting. She described the move from home and motherhood to the world of work as 'just a step in personal development'. As she said, 'You have had one era of your life – you brought up your children – and you have started another era. It's been a natural progression.' For most of the women in this study, the progression had, in fact, been far from natural, in the sense of being part of life's game plan as it might be for many career-orientated men. Indeed, earlier in the interview, Claire herself had said that her move back into full-time work had 'just happened' and that there was 'no planned progression'. Nevertheless, it is interesting that the concept of a progression was clearly part of the way Claire looked at her life – a movement through a series of roles, whether planned or not.

Authority

There was a sense in which the period in higher education had been the prelude to a series of movements, many of which have been described in the previous chapter. It was a prelude that created space for that state of narcissism and of self-examination which has been described in Chapter 5. There it was suggested that the students' response to the experience of education reflected an opposition to instrumental masculinity through a more expressive definition of the educational process. As we have seen, this now had to be negotiated in the context of work and needed to be defined in terms of the work roles that they played. Kath, for example, identified a style of management that she found acceptably feminine and appropriate to the work she did. It is not surprising, therefore, that the change in context – from the relatively contemplative life of the student to the active working life – had to some degree suppressed the anxiety and concern about the self. With one or two exceptions, those who took part in the second interview demonstrated a confidence that was only emergent during the first interview.

For most, authority was vested in knowledge or in the job itself, but for some there was more acceptance that this spilled over into personal life. This was not necessarily always for the good, however. Susan, for example, confessed to being 'bossy' at home (or rather, that's what her husband called her), but her writ did not run to exercising control over her children whose rebellious behaviour had kept her 'sane in a way'. Janet, an infant and nursery school teacher, found herself consulted by friends with children who were seeking advice, and acknowledged that she was seen as somebody who could 'see them through a difficult time'. Even so, she resisted the idea that when she discussed education with friends or relatives she was presenting herself as 'an authority figure'. Again the crossing of boundaries was seen as inappropriate and the boundaries themselves had legitimacy. Belinda, law graduate, former nurse, and subsequently a manager within the NHS found the 'overspill' from her degree sometimes awkward to handle. For example, people would expect her to offer legal advice which she felt ill-equipped to provide. In the context of her home life, she found admitting what she did rather awkward:

> I think that with people like my children's friends and people like that it does give a kind of authority which I try hard to play down. Sometimes, I find it embarrassing, and if people mention or ask what I've done, I would avoid the question.

Within the context of work, too, there was a concern to define and restrict the scope of authority. Gwen, a social worker, accepted the necessity of authority in her job, but hoped she did not abuse it. Majorie particularly expressed the need for meticulous distinctions. The presumption of authority, even at work, was for her wrong, though she confessed to allowing it to creep into her behaviour a little. More correctly she felt she should demonstrate her authority through expertise, without being 'dictatorial' and remaining open to others' suggestions. The real gain was not felt in terms of enhanced authority, but rather in terms of increased control over situations. For example, Geraldine said she now felt 'totally in control' of her own life, and Helen used the same phrase more than once, though in both cases changes in their personal lives had been as important in achieving this as education.

Lindsay and Claire, however, related control to the increased organizational complexity of their lives and whilst there clearly was a greater sense of independence on the part of many, it was seen to be contingent upon external circumstances: such as the presence or absence of encumbrances like unwanted husbands or demanding children, or demanding or stressful work. An increased sense of authority, control and confidence then were certainly in evidence, often related to an acceptance of greater role complexity in their lives. It is interesting, though, that the concept that troubled them most was, as in the first interview, still that of authority.

Gwen, a social worker, was concerned not only about the abuse of authority, but also about its effect upon relationships:

> I like to think I don't abuse it. I like to think that I value the person I am talking to as a person rather than anything else. I sincerely hope that I don't abuse the authority . . . People probably think of you as having more value in what you say . . . People defer in that way because they think that you know more than they do.

Asked about whether she felt she had more control over her life, she continued:

> Maybe it's a proof. Before I knew in myself what I was about, but having got the degree, it's proved to everybody what you are about as well, so maybe in that way it's made me have more control, other people sensing it, seeing it at work.

If Gwen expressed the complex feelings that surrounded the issue of knowledge as power, Marjorie, who had taken various management courses subsequent to her degree, expressed a more conventionally 'feminine' response:

> I think for me one of the major stumbling blocks that I had in my life was that if my head told me how to do something, then there wasn't any reason why it couldn't be done. And I think that education had a lot to contribute towards that, so that I lost touch with feelings and was more in touch with the intellect. So that that meant in practical terms, for instance, that if my head told me a job should be done in a certain way, or if it told me (after I had been on a management course) that if I adopted a certain style, I would be a certain type of manager, I would then listen to my head and put it into practice. But it was likely that my heart or my feelings would be actually telling me something quite different. That was a problem.

The knowledge she gained from management courses, she found, presented barriers to her relationships with people at work, but she drew a very sharp distinction between this and the experience of her arts-based degree, which she felt had left her with a feeling of greater faith in herself and a sense of excitement that having changed the direction of her life once she could do it again, as indeed she did in giving up her administrative post in social services to start a business. Marjorie in the end rejected the rational, instrumental world of administrative management in favour of work in a female-dominated world where personal relationships were of considerable significance. As a consequence, her interpretation of the value of her degree was very personal, but it had led her, finally, not to the world of person-orientated professionalism (where many of her fellow respondents ended up in teaching and social work) but into small-scale entrepreneurial capitalism.

Irony was to be found in Val's discussion of authority; she being one of the few to be working in the private sector as a secretary/PA, but with a sociology degree behind her. Her job she described as 'a helping role', working in a team that was under pressure but where the social relationships were good. Her response to questions about authority was interesting:

> I don't believe that the exercise of authority is just a simple question of black and white. People may come to you because they know you are educated to ask you a question about what the next course of action should be, but that sort of relationship between someone in authority and someone not in authority implies that one person is helping the other. So authority isn't just a one-way process. If you have some authority to give, you often lose more than you receive, so I don't think authority is really any big deal . . . I see life really in more spiritual terms than those. I think if you feel comfortable with yourself and you want to help somebody, whoever you are or whatever you do, if you want to help, that is far more preferable to having authority and dispensing grams of it to other people. So, I can't think of another word for [authority] . . . but it's just a sense of being comfortable with yourself and wanting to help.

If those in teaching and social work felt marginally more comfortable with the concept of authority, as least insofar as it applied to the work situation, this was perhaps because the 'personal' was enshrined and legitimated in public understanding of their job. Marjorie, though working in social services, had a purely administrative function, and Val was working in the business world. Given their educational backgrounds, perhaps they felt a greater need to explain the nature of authority in their particular work situations. As we have seen, Marjorie was about to leave her job, and it is interesting to note that Val, too, felt the pull of the social work/teaching complex. Having, through personal circumstances, been unable to undertake professional training after graduation, she did acknowledge that she was drawn to the idea of obtaining counselling or teaching English as a foreign language qualifications. Like Marjorie, however, she was also attracted by the idea of working for herself, rather than for an employer. One or two of the teachers, it should be noted, did cite the autonomy their work offered as a clear asset.

Class

It was suggested in Chapter 5 that the class trajectory of these women was into the enclave of the new middle class, and unsurprisingly, this is where most of those involved in the second interview ended up. Culturally, they inhabited the expressive rather than the instrumental end of the spectrum – the place where 'feminine' interpretations of the world are most easily accepted. We have noted a certain unease being expressed in the second interview about the more managerial aspects of work, and in these discussions about status, authority and control a degree of ambivalence was still in evidence. Gender clearly had a great deal to do with this and amongst our respondents, Kath specifically identified gender as an issue in management style.

Though the size of the group and the nature of the evidence we have is very restricted, the question of class should not be ignored completely. New class theory is a fragmented and undeveloped aspect of class theory, but in Gouldner's formulation, supported by the work of Bernstein, it does offer ways of exploring the class position of the women in this study, albeit in a very tentative and provisional way. Bernstein identified the new middle class as one associated primarily with the processes of cultural repro-duction, as the 'regulators', 'repairers', 'diffusers', 'shapers' and 'executors' of modern Western societies, and he saw their conflict with the old middle class as being based upon an alternative conception of organic solidarity, where the concept of the person holds sway over the concept of the individual (Bernstein, 1975: 100). Gouldner saw a class with a role not dissimilar to that suggested by Bernstein, a knowledge class including those whose task is to provide the technology of reproduction as well as that of production. Consequently he saw a class itself internally divided between those espousing a humanist tradition and those in pursuit of rationality through technology (Gouldner, 1979). Whilst the importance of class to gender studies has been well established by writers such as Arnot and Weiler, these particular ideas have not, to our knowledge, been thoroughly explored (Arnot, 1982,1984; Weiler, 1988). This is, perhaps, somewhat surprising given the close historical relationship between women and cultural reproduction. There is also the cultural association of women with what Martin (1981) calls the expressive enclave and of men with the instrumental; dimensions of society that can easily be related to Gouldner's humanist and technocratic traditions. Bernstein, it will be recalled, identified the contradictory class position of those who, pursuing the concept of the person, espoused the counter-cultural form of organic solidarity. In Chapter 5 we suggested that, on leaving the world of the student, these women would face a degree of conflict between the cultural position they espoused as students and the instrumental, rational world that lay beyond the safe haven of higher education.

Here we can only suggest some very tentative conclusions in relation to our group of respondents. First, that the potential conflict had been reduced insofar as the women interviewed for the second time, especially the teachers and social workers, had found a relatively safe home in classic new-middle-class jobs. Even given the current political hostility to much of what they did, these at least offered a formal and public legitimation for many of the ideas and beliefs they had espoused as students. Secondly, there was evidence of some compromise: an acceptance of the special experience of student life, which in the 'real' world had to accommodate to the different roles that human beings, and perhaps women especially, were called upon to play. The fragmentation of the self and the 'boundary' problems this created were now accepted as practical problems to be dealt with; indeed, on occasions, it could be an advantage. Thirdly, a sense of unease, especially about questions of status and authority had remained with them and caused some difficulties both in relation to work itself and also in terms of the complexity of roles this produced, causing 'bossiness' at home, and creating demands to provide advice and help.

Gender and class clearly interact here, but the evidence of this study casts only a very faint light upon the dynamics of the process. Geraldine provided an interesting example of the contradictions of the situation. She had drifted into her degree in accounting and maths, felt unhappy working in accountancy, being unable to take to 'the professional office-type syndrome', and was drawn back into education and eventually into a teaching post in her old department. But the influences she experienced upon the way are instructive. To begin with, she was never convinced that this was the right degree for her. Presumably because of her earlier work in a bank she had been encouraged to take accountancy and to think in terms of a future career in the private sector. But the advice she received, she felt, took her along 'the wrong paths' and her subsequent experience of working in accountancy practice was obviously unhappy and tedious, and not helped by the fact that, as a trainee, she was so badly paid. She had never thought of teaching as a career but was 'elbowed' into thinking of teaching by friends and acquaintances, most of whom, she said, were teachers; they, she thought, had been the biggest influence upon her since she graduated. Gender, however, also played its part in her experience. It seemed not to have played a part in her choice of degree, but when she started work she experienced problems as a single parent. Working as a teacher in higher education gave her a much more interesting and congenial social milieu in which to work, but it was still, of course (being a department of business studies), dominated by men, or by women less harassed by family demands. In addition she experienced the increasingly 'macho' style of management prevalent in higher education as a major source of frustration, exacerbated by the fact that having been a student in the same department she could remember what it was like to have been taught there some years earlier. For Geraldine, the public and private sectors, the instrumental and the expressive milieux, the macho and the caring were tangled together in a contradictory and complex web:

> This one (job) is certainly more of a career than working in the professional office. That was certainly a job, just a job, to get a salary at the end. This current one [teaching in HE] . . . I don't really know. I'm dithering about it at the moment. I find it very difficult, the way things are today, to make a career out of it. Every time you try and push forward, something knocks you back . . . we've had all these new contracts imposed on us and all sorts of things. It's very hard not to treat it just as a job, to be perfectly honest . . . just treat it as a job and then you won't get upset by it.

Geraldine's aspiration was for a vocation offering involvement with other people at a personal level. Her need was to get out of debt and earn sufficient money to keep her household together. In seeking to resolve her problems, she seemed to have faced cultural conflicts related to both class and gender.

Social distance

One of the key concepts in Boudon's theory relates to the sense of social distance that an individual perceives it to be necessary to travel to obtain a particular objective; an aspect of the so-called 'secondary effects' (Boudon, 1973/4). This idea is one that has particular relevance to this group of women. We had, after the second interview, evidence relating to the whole of their educational lives. Much of it was given retrospectively during the first interview, but contained considerable detail about their past experiences and expectations of education as they left school. In the same interview they had talked at length about their feelings as students in higher education, and subsequently in the second interview they were given the opportunity to reflect upon that experience. In particular they were asked to what extent they felt the experience of being a student (and, by implication, of all that had happened to them during a period of major decision-making in their lives) had been a transforming one. Their response to this gave us some measure of the social distance they felt they had travelled, and of the impact that education had had upon them.

Rather than attempt to summarize their responses, it seems more appropriate to illustrate the range of answers with a few case studies of individuals. Since what is important is life history, the educational origins and destinations of particular individuals are presented here. As we indicated when discussing their educational histories, these women were not representative of the general population. They were relatively well educated, and frequently their education had been disrupted rather than reaching a natural close; or, at least, they subsequently interpreted it in this way. In this sense they fitted well the pattern anticipated for mature students by Hopper and Osborn, who emphasized the subjective feelings mature students had about the impersonal workings of the educational system (Hopper and Osborn, 1975). What we also thought we detected was a feeling by some of our respondents that their own parents had had educational careers that had been thwarted in some way. Whether this sense of disruption (in the case of either our group of women or their parents) was objectively true is only partially relevant; what was important was the subjective sense of deprivation. This was associated with gender, with what was expected of girls at school, with events related to boyfriends and marriage, and with feelings about their early jobs. This they expressed quite clearly. We also detected in their responses an uneasiness about class position and aspirations, which, though they did not articulate it explicitly, acted as a barrier to their ability to see opportunities. Later, what became more important in the careers of these women was to challenge the determining force of gender. Hence what might have been interpreted by an older generation as stabilizing – marriage, 'female' employment, a good but limited education – became reinterpreted as interferences or hindrances to a more fulfilled life, or, in the context of the changing environment of marriage, as an impediment to the economic survival of their household.

Class and educational mobility were a feature of the careers of these women as was a changing attitude to gender. As we have described earlier, their parents generally had had very little education beyond school, but almost a third of those we could identify had been to selective schools. In occupational terms the parents were located predominantly in manual or lower-middle-class occupations. In respect to dimensions of class, education and gender, a certain social distance had been travelled, and the brief case studies that follow attempt to trace that social distance and to indicate the women's feelings about the effect the journey had upon them. Though each was a very individual experience, they do convey some sense both of the shared experiences and of the very considerable differences between individuals whose points of departure and whose life histories were very varied.

Dorcas

To start with Dorcas is to be reminded that not all these stories are tales of rags to riches success. Born at the beginning of the Second World War to parents who had both had a grammar school education and some subsequent vocational training, Dorcas herself went to grammar school. Her father had his own business and her mother was a secretary. Dorcas was taking four A levels at school and intending to study medicine when a distraction appeared in the shape of a steady boyfriend whom she wanted to marry. Her parents (her mother especially) were not enthusiastic and the compromise reached was for her to drop all but one A level and to abandon medicine for teacher training, which she duly did. It is clear, however, that some sort of further education was assumed, both by Dorcas herself, her parents and her school friends. She married at the age of 21. Her younger brother went to university and later qualified as a solicitor.

The choice of teaching was made because it was thought it would 'fit in with marriage and children'. She taught full time for a few years, then when her children were born she had a period of being a full-time mother and housewife. At the age of 33 she went back to part-time work, but found it difficult to reconcile her work with what she perceived to be her responsibilities at home. She did, however, successfully complete an A level course in psychology just before she separated from her husband at the age of 37. At this point she began to feel the need to 'develop' herself, to, as she put it, 'really immerse myself in something that would take all my concentration'. Despite an initially discouraging response to her enquiries as a mature student she was eventually accepted to study for a degree in psychology. The interest in psychology was significant because it developed, she said, during her teacher training. It was also perhaps as close to the study of medicine as she could hope to get in her new circumstances. Her mother was anxious about this interest because she felt it would make her daughter even more introspective than she already believed her to be. Dorcas's commitment to psychology, as a subject, however, was obviously very strong.

An additional and significant factor in this decision to seek another qualification was a deteriorating physical disability that made class teaching increasingly difficult, a factor that eventually allowed her, after considerable argument, to obtain a grant.

After one year of her degree, Dorcas had to suspend her course because of family difficulties when the behaviour of one of her children became a problem. During this period she remarried, whereupon she recalled that her friends and her parents assumed that she would not need to resume her course, believing she 'should be content to be someone's wife'. Nobody seemed to appreciate, she complained, that her studies were 'the most stimulating thing' she had ever done and that now she wanted to 'find her own place in life', to be financially independent and to have her own 'professional niche'. Her husband's family, though not voicing its opposition, seemed to feel sympathy with the husband for having 'such an undomesticated and untypical wife'. Ironically, the financial independence that she had sought was compromised by her marriage because her grant was cut and her children became dependent upon their stepfather. Whilst he raised no objection, she clearly felt uncomfortable with the situation and was never quite able to overcome the sense of guilt at not being a 'proper' mother, or indeed, as her parents grew older, a proper daughter.

As a student she was clearly far from quiescent, filing complaints about parts of the course, but deeply involved in her work, especially those parts of it that allowed her to work on her own. Indeed, initially uncertain of what was expected of her, she spent far more time on each assignment than her fellow students. She was also far more argumentative in tutorials, but was surprised to find her contributions accepted as valuable by her tutors.

She graduated with what was clearly a good degree since she was asked if she wanted to take a research degree. However, what she had really wanted to do was to become a clinical psychologist, but she discovered that she was too old to be accepted for training. She decided not to pursue research because she still felt the conflict between being a student and a wife; to carry on as a student she did not think would be 'fair'. She also felt tied to the local area, and family complications were never far below the surface. The search for work was frustrating, turning her into a 'professional applicant', seeking 80 to 90 jobs after completing her degree. She obtained a number of part-time jobs, some as a research assistant and some as a psychologist, but gradually moved towards counselling, for which she began a course that would give her some accreditation. She had deliberately not told anybody on the course that she had a degree, because she thought they might feel she had an 'unfair advantage', which, though it would not be her 'fault', would have made her feel embarrassed.

Dorcas's decision to return to higher education and to take a degree had a number of consequences. It gave her back the educational status, relative to her school friends, which she had abandoned for marriage, but it had few external benefits, least of all in terms of jobs. Her parents clearly had very ambiguous attitudes towards education and careers for their daughter, prizing education itself perhaps, but not its consequences in terms of its effect upon women's careers and attitudes to family life. For their generation, this was not untypical, but its consequences clearly dogged Dorcas for much of her life. Unfortunately, her children were not encouraged by their mother's intellectual prowess and though the son did continue into higher education, Dorcas felt, particularly with her daughter, that the effect of mother spending hours with her books had been very negative. The attitude of neither husband was terribly clear, but that of the surrounding penumbra of families seemed not to have been positive.

There are three dimensions along which one might measure the social distance Dorcas travelled; personal educational fulfilment, a revised sense of gender role, and upward social and economic mobility. In terms of the last, there was clearly very little movement and little sense that she had moved into a different social milieu; hers was a middle-class world and remained so, though there was the characteristic shift from father's business world to her own world of teaching, research and counselling. The search for financial independence was frustrating and eventually fruitless, as the factor of age increasingly reduced her opportunities in the labour market. There was no information offered about husbands' occupations, but little indication that they shared her particular occupational world.

The gender dimension was clearly the most fraught, with the change in role producing feelings of guilt that she was never able to resolve. Teaching as a career might have been acceptable, both to parents and to children, as an established women's job, though even that Dorcas found difficult to manage. Clearly, the constraints were material as well as emotional, but the ascribed gender role was one she felt unable to challenge radically.

The biggest change was in her final achievement of the educational status that her schooling had predicted for her. Hers was not a move into unknown territory in the way that it was for many of these women, but rather a final achievement of what had been expected of her as a schoolgirl. The sense of personal achievement was unaffected by subsequent disappointments and the moment of being 'supremely happy' at graduation was still with her, as was the sense of confidence that achievement had given her. What Dorcas did not do, however, was to interpret this success as a change in her role as a woman and though, objectively, it is easy to see the influence of gender upon her educational career, the fact that she did not see it in those terms was probably the biggest factor limiting the distance she could move along the gender dimension. The concept of social distance implies not only objective movements, but also their subjective interpretation. Another, more 'feminist' woman might have interpreted the situation differently, and might consequently have been able to travel much further. However, it must also be said that the constraints of age, disability and family circumstance were very considerable and it would be hard, and certainly improper, for any outsider to challenge the rationality of the individual decisions she made.

Kath

Kath came from what she described as a working-class background. Her father had learned a trade in the Royal Air Force and subsequently worked as a technician in a college; her mother worked as a hairdresser and as a cook with, apparently, a long period of being a mother and housewife without paid employment. In terms of schooling, she described her father's education as 'ordinary', but her mother, coming from a middle class background, had been to some kind of selective school that had had an entrance examination. Her mother's brother had been to university and successfully completed a PhD. According to Kath, her uncle's education had been seen as much more important than that of her mother who had been steered towards traditional female roles. Of Kath's two sisters, one had been to grammar school and thence to teacher training, but had worked in a bank both before and after having her children; the other sister had been to a non-selective secondary school and thence to hairdressing and briefly to running her own business. At the time of the first interview, however, this sister was in her third year on a course training as an occupational therapist.

Kath's own secondary education consisted of a couple of years at a secondary modern from where she went, having passed some exams, to an art school which was promptly closed as part of the reorganisation of the local schools into comprehensives in the late 1960s. She transferred to what she described as a 'technical' school, but never settled being only ever interested in art, and left without any qualifications at the age of 15. At this point she seems to have entered a period when romance and cosy images of domesticity dominated her life, marrying at 17 and having children soon after; her brief experience of work before marriage seems to have done little to encourage her to think of work as a place for personal satisfaction or development. Eight years as a housewife and mother living in a council house seem to have been fraught with economic, practical and emotional difficulties. It was an experience she herself described as 'an extremely working-class existence' and one from which she felt she learned a great deal, but which left her feeling isolated and frustrated.

Economic problems, and the difficulties her husband had in obtaining a steady income, eventually drove her to seek work, and one particular day in a chocolate factory seems to have forced her to think more radically about a change in her life. Seeing an advertisement about training in a job centre and then plucking up the courage to walk through the doors of a local college of further education was the beginning. From there she went through O levels and A levels to undergraduate and postgraduate degrees, including professional training as a social worker. With these qualifications she achieved rapid promotion to middle management jobs within social services. Her parents and children appear to have been approving and supportive. The marriage contracted so young, however, seems not to have survived. During her undergraduate days Kath described her husband as supportive, but experiencing difficulty in coping with a wife who was rapidly and radically changing her life.

In terms of the three dimensions of social distance used to discuss Dorcas's situation, a somewhat different picture emerges here. As far as economic and social mobility is concerned there was considerable movement, initially down upon her marriage and then up into the middle management ranks of a public sector organization. There were, however, one or two interesting staging posts along the way. Clearly, the first move back into education was the most dramatic, but after her undergraduate degree there was a period of stock-taking, working within the social services field, before embarking upon professional training and a more career-orientated life. At the time of the second interview, there was again a sense of taking stock, of needing to decide very carefully whether a move into the higher echelons of management was what she really aspired to.

We have noted that some of the women in the second interview appeared to have held back from full-blooded pursuit of their careers, because some, like Felicity for example, disliked the 'pushiness' that had to accompany the quest for promotion. Kath discussed this at some length in her second interview, identifying very clearly that she felt there was a price to be paid in terms of behaviour, the way one dressed (jumper and jeans were her normal work clothes) and in attitude, if one wished to enter the 'macho' world of senior management. What Kath also did was to articulate this problem in terms of gender and to define the particular position she had already achieved as one where a more feminine style was appropriate and acceptable. This, she said, she was reluctant to leave. It is, however, possible to see this also in class terms, as part of the conflict between the role orientated behaviour Bernstein suggests is characteristic of the old bourgeoisie and the more personalized presentation of the integrated self to which the new class aspires. The expressive, 'feminine' culture of new class aspirations, may be sustainable at middle management levels within organizations such as social services, but the visibility of senior management jobs to the world outside renders them more susceptible to the pressures of the old tradition. It may be that for some of the women in this study, including Kath, gender and the cultural aspiration of new class combined to place some restraint upon career aspirations.

Kath was one of the most 'feminist' of our respondents, and the dimension of gender was one along which she showed the greatest awareness of having moved. Hers was a very self-conscious articulation of the changes that took place in her attitudes, from romantic, teenage, working-class aspiration for husband, house and children to an appreciation of economic reality and of the limitations of the domestic dream. Unlike most of these women, she seemed to have found relatively little fulfilment even in motherhood, whilst work seemed to have provided the first real focus for satisfaction as she shaped a successful career for herself after graduation.

As far as education itself was concerned, it might look on first inspection as if Kath represented a classic case of a girl leaving school with nothing, but achieving educational success through fierce individual motivation, assisted by an enlightened further education college and university. On closer inspection however, it can be seen that she also provides evidence of the power of both the Hopper/Osborn thesis and that of Boudon. In her family background are traces of educational opportunities fulfilled and frustrated. Her own mother she interpreted as having had educational ambitions curtailed by an ascribed gender role, whilst her mother's brother went on to graduate and postgraduate study. Additionally, she had one sister who had trained as a teacher, though without practising her profession, and another sister who, after an undistinguished school career, had, at much the same time as Kath, gone back to train as an occupational therapist. Thus in terms of the Hopper/Osborn thesis one might argue that there was enough in her background to make the 'cooling out' process problematic, and in terms of Boudon's third dimension, it is clear that although she left school without qualifications, her circumstances were different from those of many working-class girls who left school at a similar time in a similar way. There was enough in her background to provide the motivation and, perhaps most importantly, to enable her to visualize a future as an educated woman – to look across the social distance from her past to her future. In this respect she represents a characteristic manifested in individual ways by many of the women in this study.

Jean

Jean was amongst the most diffident of our respondents, and one of the few who found it really difficult to recall the feelings and attitudes important to her when she left school. She described herself frequently as shy and inarticulate, though she talked with some freedom about her work during the second interview. In studies such as this, people like Jean are liable to disappear beneath the more extrovert and self-consciously articulate who offer so many more 'quotable quotes'; but for our discussion of social distance her story is interesting and worth recounting.

She was born during the Second World War to parents who split up soon afterwards; of her father she knew almost nothing since her mother broke off all contact. Her mother remarried and had three more children, but Jean seems to have spent most of her childhood with her widowed grandmother and not with her step-family. She did, however, spend her last year at school there, which on reflection she felt had not been a good idea. When she was first working in her teens she had a bed-sit in the house of an uncle, her grandmother having, by then, given up her own home. There would seem to have been little in the way of formal education in her family background. Her mother worked as a shop assistant and manager-ess; her half-siblings either in banking (sister, very briefly) or in skilled manual jobs (brothers). She herself went to a prestigious girls-only, selective, direct-grant secondary school where she described herself as middle of the road in terms of achievement. She had assumed that, along with the majority of her peers, she would go on into the sixth form and it was in her mind that she might train as a teacher. But when the time came she left at 16. Her mother thought education was a waste for girls who were going to get married and have children, and Jean clearly looked with a certain amount of envy at those neighbourhood friends from junior school who had not gone to grammar school and who were then earning. There had been friends at grammar school with parents from professional backgrounds, but their influence proved insufficient against the assump-tions and expectations of home and neighbourhood.

She worked in a small bank, a lone teenager amongst chivalrous but distant middle-aged men. She described herself as very shy of boys, brought up by a grandmother who was 'anti-men' and regarded by her family as only ever likely to have cats. At 20, however, she married a man she had known as a schoolgirl and in her mid-twenties she had two children. Soon, however, she was attending evening classes, initially non-vocational courses; then in her early thirties, because she could not get on to a German class, she took an economics course. This led to an O level, and thence over a period of some five years to A levels and to the start of a university degree in history. Meanwhile she had been working part time as a library assistant, and this was the career she pursued after graduation, achieving professional status after a considerable struggle. At the time of the second interview she held a responsible job as a medical librarian. For reasons she did not disclose, she was then the main breadwinner for her household.

In terms of distance travelled along the socio-economic continuum, Jean's origins are uncertain. She lived with her grandmother, but the material circumstances of her life are unclear. Her mother worked as a shop assistant and manageress: her step-sister worked only very briefly and her step brothers, though initially entering skilled trades, apparently 'drifted', to use Jean's own word. In Jean's own married household, there were a few suggestions of economic struggle, though not on the scale of Kath's. Once she did outwork, but rejected it as 'slave labour', and though later she worked part-time as a librarian, it seems not to have been primarily for economic reasons. She was possibly marginally upwardly mobile from childhood to adult life, but a distinct shift in terms of status if not material circumstances, came after she finally achieved professional status as a librarian running, with the help of her own library assistant, a medical library service within the health service. At the time of the second interview she was on the edge of further development of her career and in the process of looking for jobs. However, she was restricted in her ambitions both by household circumstances and by a lack of confidence in her own abilities, and as with Kath and Dorcas, though for different reasons, she reflects that rather complex relationship to career which was discussed in the last chapter.

In terms of gender, Jean presented herself at the first interview as one of the most conservative, particularly in seeing biological differences behind the different choice of subjects of men and women. She rejected the idea that gender might have affected her career prospects after leaving school, and hinted at a certain dislike of feminism. It is also interesting that in her teens, because of her shyness and her grandmother's hostility to men, she seemed to see a spinster future for herself, probably as a teacher. Her family would appear to have endorsed this with their comments about cats. She shared with many of our respondents the experience of the contrast between the reality and the image of marriage, but in her case, given the unusual nature of her upbringing, this may have been intensified. Her remarks about motherhood, however, amongst the many positive comments we received, were amongst the most enthusiastic, and she was particularly involved in her children's early education, going into school to help with reading. It was in her postgraduate career as a librarian, however, that she met and acknowledged the existence of discrimination, recounting how one doctor expected her to be his typist and how others compared her office favourably to that of the medical secretaries, assuming that she herself must be one such. How much of her shyness and continuing feelings of inarticulacy could be related back to gender, it is clearly impossible to gauge with any precision, but it is difficult to escape the impression that the shy teenager who would cross the road rather than meet a boy, whilst undoubtedly having travelled a long way in terms of confidence in the public arena, still carried with her a residue of uncertainty.

Jean's educational history identifies another pattern of some interest. Immediately upon leaving school and entering employment, she realized that she had made a mistake, but given her educational isolation at home she felt she had no one to turn to; an attempt to explain the situation to a careers officer apparently produced no response. In contrast to Kath, for example, it was school rather than family that sowed the seeds of educational aspiration, and it is interesting that she consistently interpreted educational value in purely personal terms; this in spite of having achieved postgraduate and professional qualifications as a librarian. She presented all her learning as 'selfish', to do with her sense of curiosity and self fulfilment, as being the 'need within myself'. Her husband was not pleased about her entry to higher education, though he appeared to have accepted it and there seemed to be no external motivation in the shape of economic necessity. It is, of course, speculation, but it is interesting to ponder whether it was the relative insularity of her experience of education in a prestigious direct-grant school, coupled with her own very obvious shyness, that produced this very introverted view of the value of education. Having said that, however, it is important to appreciate that Jean, albeit in a particularly marked fashion, suggested an attitude to education that, as we have argued in Chapter 5, was very common amongst these women. Learning was not for exhibition, it was not part of a cultural display, rather it was an aspect of a belief in the capacity of the human mind, through intellectual exercise, to change and reshape human experience. As Jean herself said:

> It's bound to change you, the process of education, you look at things differently, you appreciate things more, I think it's a sad fact of life, the less education you have, the less you are able to appreciate the good things in life . . . education is for life . . . it's a permanent process.

Jean provides the testimonial in the 1990s for those educational reformers of the 1960s who dreamed of educational opportunity coming through schooling and rescuing the working classes from their cultural dreariness. From the perspective of the 1990s the vision looks naive and patronizing, but those radicals of 30 years ago could take some comfort from the fact that many of these women, albeit rarely displaying total educational deprivation in their backgrounds, nevertheless so often experienced the lure and excitement of using their minds to change the world. Perhaps Jean, battling against a difficult childhood, an inauspicious educational environment outside school, an unsupportive husband, and a life in which career aspirations never figured very large, should have the last word on the feelings of our mature students about education:

> Even if I had been guaranteed that I wouldn't be doing anything at the end of it, I don't think that would have deterred me. It was the goal. I enjoyed studying and I just wanted to learn more and I enjoyed my subject. At the time it was to get through the degree and then the next

step. I sometimes think of that fairy story of the old lady who reached for the moon; each thing she got she wanted something more. So I really ought to be satisfied now with what I have.

Education is, however, as she admits a 'compulsion'.

8
Conclusion

Reproduction

There seems a measure of contradiction between the work of women theorizing about education and the accounts that these particular women students gave of their lives and the place of education within them.

Theorists have focused on educational institutions as reproducing the structures that are oppressive to women; they have seen domesticity and low-paid work as the end-point of the educational process. Where empirical work in this tradition has studied the experience of girls, it has tended to take the position that girls' rejection of schools' definition of themselves has taken a form such as romance that ultimately guarantees their subordination (McRobbie, 1978). In this way girls become implicated in the reproduction of femininity.

The women in our study saw education as the starting point of a new process: as a way of breaking out of domesticity, low-paid work and the mesh in which low-paid work, women's careers and domesticity ensnared them. At the time of the first interviews, they were not in doubt: education was going to increase their opportunity in the world of paid work; increase their independence from traditional family structures; ensure their survival in the case where those family structures had broken down, and give them a new identity where the domestic one had failed.

These women's perceptions of the role of education in their lives bear much more resemblance to notions of education as opportunity, expressed by the early pioneers of education for women (and latterly by Blackstone (1987)) than they do to those of most feminist theorists of the nature of education for women and girls today.

There seem several ways of coming to understand this apparent contradiction between researchers viewing education as an aspect of women's oppression, and women students seeing it as opportunity.

First, theories of reproduction have often been preoccupied with structures, with the contexts and restrictions that frame the lives of girls and women. The women in our study were reflecting on their life histories. They acknowledged in some measure the restrictions of the various structures they encountered, but their focus on life history led them to emphasize the strategies they had employed in tracing their way through. Some of the disparity, then, might be understood as a difference of perspective: women researchers were concentrating on the structures, while the mature women students were focused on more individual activity. But it may still be noted that where theories of reproduction have taken girls' own experience as the focus, it has made the picture more complex, but has sometimes led to the same conclusion: girls are seen as complicit in the adoption of strategies that will lead them into low-paid work and motherhood.

Another – and related – way of looking at the contradiction is to see our respondents as misguided. Structures may be visible to those within them, but then again they may not. We had a graphic example of this in a part of the interview that asked about work histories. We asked whether being a woman had affected the experience of paid work. The respondent who answered, 'No, I was doing women's work you see', encapsulated this point. She and the others who answered this way illustrated the overwhelming importance of gender as a structural variable affecting employment. But at the same time they did not feel the impact of these structural forces in their day-to-day lives. Doing women's work and working alongside women may indeed insulate women from the experience of discrimination, even while it confirms their restricted place in the job market. A teacher who acknowledged that men were in charge, while saying that she did not experience discrimination, made the same point. 'I taught mainly in junior school where there were always a lot of women and so I was accepted, although headmasters tend to be headmasters, I think women are accepted as equals.'

We could go on to argue that the oppressive structures of education were equally invisible to the women in them; that their search for an escape from domesticity and low-paid work through education was misguided. However, in most respects, awareness of the structures that constrained respondents' lives was acute. Experience in the labour market and the family gave them a very clear perception of wage structures and domestic work, if not always of the discriminatory processes in employment. Respondents were well experienced in educational institutions and processes by the time of the interviews, and there was nothing in the interviews that suggested that educational structures might be setting them a trap; on the contrary, faith and hope were almost tangible. Experience bore them out. By the time of the second interviews, the majority of respondents were established in careers, and those who were not put the blame elsewhere than on education – on discrimination at work, family pressures, lack of mobility and so on.

Thirdly, it should be remarked that most writing about educational structures is about schooling rather than education. There is an emphasis on school discipline and hierarchy, on curriculum and set texts. We should ask whether women returning to study as adults have such a different experience of educational structures that they should be set outside the debate about the nature of education for girls and treated as an exceptional group.

The literature on gender and education has had rather little to say about adults or higher education. MacDonald in 1980 rather depressingly saw women as future 'domestic pedagogues'! Jane Thompson's account of the history of adult education is equally depressing: 'Apart from the Co-operative Guilds and the women's trade unions, there is little evidence of education concerned with anything other than basic accommodation to the sexual division of labour in the home, and the transmission of skills commensurate with the requirements of capital for cheap, unskilled secondary labour' (Thompson, 1983), though her title, *Learning Liberation*, indicates more optimism for present and future. Acker and Piper's title *Is Higher Education Fair to Women?* (1984) also implies that higher education is something that women might reasonably want.

The women in this study had in fact two different experiences of education. Their first experience as schoolgirls had equipped them variously for paid employment. It had given some no basis at all for work that would sustain roof, life and health, and others a basis for a career; it had led nearly all to a ghetto of female work that proved unsustainable as a long-term career or source of economic support. It may not be unconnected that for most of our respondents, school was also followed by domesticity. Schools may well have played their part in developing these patterns and expectations of women's domestic lives. But we should also remember that these expectations have other sources in family and culture, and our respondents did not convict schools of this particular crime.

Women returning to higher education have more control than schoolgirls, more freedom to take what they can use out of education and leave the rest. Our respondents' second experience of educational institutions differed in many respects from their earlier one. But their choice of education as a route for future development suggests that they did not see it as necessarily preparing them for domestic life, even if it had fulfilled that role in the past. The majority view was of its necessary role in the development of new and more sustainable careers.

There is little in this study that can shed light on theories of education in relation to girls. But it seems safer to look for theories that can accommodate the variety of women's experience of education, including that of mature students, than to treat this growing group as an exception to a general rule. As Blackstone has indicated and as the increased qualifications levels of girls at school leaving testifies, education does offer women opportunities; and the credentialist tie between work and education is as strong for women as it is for men. One thing this study suggests is that as returners to education these women 'remembered' an experience of schooling as holding possibilities.

Fourthly, it is possible to incorporate particular groups in a general theory of reproduction as minorities. Escape from domesticity for a few women via education may be a way of co-opting the most dissatisfied, thus legitimating the position of the great majority. For this majority education continues to be seen as overwhelmingly preoccupied with sustaining the domestic roles of women. However, for this interpretation to be plausible, the minority has to be seen as emerging from the majority: working class children in grammar schools, for example, could be seen as a reference group for the much larger group of working-class children left out. This is not a very plausible account in this case where the women stand demographically apart from the main recipients of educational provision. They cannot therefore easily be seen as a reference group for younger women and girls in educational institutions.

Finally, it could be argued that the theories can be seen as over-deterministic, over-generalized, too little aware of the potential of those within the system, and their active role in using the system for their own ends. That they should be inclined that way is perhaps not surprising given the general theoretical stance of much educational sociology of the 1970s, and the pervasive influence of what Halsey once called Marxist func-tionalism (Karabel and Halsey, 1977). Much feminist research has es-poused qualitative methodology, as superior to the 'masculinist' tendencies of quantification in its capacity to understand the world from the subject's point of view and to explore complex social processes, but for some time accepted relatively uncritically the constraining parameters of some Marxist and quasi-Marxist theorizing. Davies quite rightly took Paul Willis to task for his ponderous male use of adjectives such as 'fundamental' and 'essential', but she might well have extended her strictures more widely to encompass the language of reproduction theory itself (Davies, 1985: 88). Whilst those at the leading edge of academic discussion may well have moved beyond such formulations, it is far from certain that, in the broader political context of feminist discussions of education, this has happened. The political weight of reproduction theories tends to militate against their more sophisticated formulations.

We should not forget the historical drama of women's fight for education. The development of schools and colleges for women, and their fight for admission to the universities were a vital part of the feminist politics of the late nineteenth century (Kamm, 1965); as Arnot indicates, 'one of the greatest women's struggles has been fought over the right of access to and social mobility through the educational system' (Arnot, 1984: 74). Neither should we dismiss the contemporary activities of women teachers (Weiler, 1988), many of whom have worked from a feminist perspective to challenge traditional perceptions of their pupils' future roles. We need at least to modify reproduction theory as an all-embracing account of what happens in education systems if we are to have any grasp of why women have felt in the past – and feel in the present – that they can achieve personal and social change through education.

The evidence of our sample of women returning to higher education is that their early life histories followed the pattern of their contemporaries: the norm was of school leaving followed by routine work or a women's career followed by a break for children (though domesticity was often mixed with courses and part-time employment). Schools may well have played a part in establishing this pattern. But it was to education that women turned to escape from the web in which many felt caught – looking for income and a career that could be combined with domestic responsibilities.

Education was not associated with a rejection of domesticity. Our respondents placed education within the context of lives in which responsibility for others, particularly children, was assumed as a priority. To that extent it can be argued that neither of their two educational phases had undermined traditional values or provided women with a means to escape the duties that go with them.

A key social change described in our respondents' life histories was of changing patterns of women's employment for which their earlier educational history had not fitted them. The domestic model of femininity may well have been the dominant one during their earlier educational careers, but it is not the only one available to those within educational institutions. It may well be losing its saliency with changes in women's employment patterns. This is not in any way to suggest that women are no longer doing domestic or caring work, but rather that the housewife role has moved into a different relationship with paid work roles to become a less dominant identity in most younger women's lives. It would be surprising if educational institutions did not reflect this.

The evidence of the second interviews bore out the optimism and aspirations of the earlier ones. Not all stories were of uncomplicated success in developing new careers; and the most successful careers were not meteoric. But most respondents had found the place in public life that they had feared closed to them. Education had played a key role in enabling new choices to be made about the balance between private and public life.

There is no shortage of evidence about the position of men in the power structures of education, and every reason to suppose that power is wielded to sustain men's privileges – in which women's domestic role plays a part. For these reasons the critical edge of the reproduction thesis must be acknowledged. Educational institutions are not simply opportunity factories. But it needs to be modified: reproduction must be seen as contested. It is not then incompatible to acknowledge that the extension of education for women and by women is a concession with real potential for destabilizing traditional notions of femininity and the dependence they sustain; or to acknowledge that our respondents were not deceiving themselves in the enthusiasm with which they grasped their opportunity.

Education theory and mature students

The general line of development of theory relating to gender and education has been in the exploration and modification of theories of reproduction, but we were drawn also towards the currently less fashionable systems-orientated theories, not least because they keep the selective function of the educational process at the forefront, and our mature students had undergone lifetimes of selection as they inched their way back to the mainstream of education. It is, above all, important to remember that any resistance by women to the hegemony of gender or of class that makes use of education, will subject them to the processes of selection that are inherent in mass educational systems. Indeed, we have argued that to the extent to which changes in gender role in the late twentieth century liberate women from traditional expectations, the more they will be incorporated into the mainstream selective function of education. The re-adjustments that this required were an important aspect of the experience of our respondents.

We introduced the issue of decision making in the introduction as part of a discussion about the more general problem of 'over-socialized' conceptions of human behaviour. In particular, we borrowed from Heath the concept of the 'impossible situation' to describe the situation where one course of action cannot rationally be preferred to another (Heath, 1974). Later on we characterized the process of decision making that led to our respondents return to education as a 'science of muddling through'. This last phrase, of course, was first used in the late 1950s by the political scientist Charles Lindblom in a critique of rational, synoptic models of policy making, but it has a peculiar appropriateness to the circumstances of these women (Lindblom, 1959, 1979). Lindblom describes a world where history shapes the future leaving space for only incremental changes, where decisions are endlessly reactive and serial, responding to an ever-changing, uncertain environment. If we wished for a theory that saw decision making as gendered, then Lindblom would provide a good starting point for describing the decision-making environment of many women.

Class is a relevant factor here of course, but few women have the opportunities afforded to some men to plan their lives in two critical areas – those of education and career. In some areas of women's lives, the environment is becoming increasingly uncertain. A still expanding educational system intent, particularly in Britain in the 1990s, on testing, profiling and evaluating from reception to leaving class and beyond, must incorporate women more and more into its mainstream purpose of selection and certification. But the surrounding culture remains sharply gendered, both in the private world of the family and in the world of work, and without a doubt this still penetrates and distorts the world of education. In addition both domesticity and work offer increasingly uncertain options and possibilities; marriage becomes partnership and potentially less constraining but more fragile; and work offers more opportunities but in the context of an increasingly deregulated labour market. These uncertainties must increase the number of impossible situations women face, where social structure does not determine a 'rational' decision. In this context a grasp of the 'science of muddling through' becomes an asset, and as pioneers the women in our study have learned both its necessity and its virtues. As Lindblom was always keen to tell his critics, muddling through is neither necessarily passive nor conservative in its implications; it indicates rather a shrewd judgement of both past and possible futures. Our respondents were by most criteria successful exponents of this science by the time they completed their degrees, not in the sense of dominating their environment, but in having gained a sharper sense of their position within it.

Decision making is, Lindblom claims, an incremental process and its study therefore requires a diachronic rather than a synchronic approach. We were fortunate in this study in being able to interview half of our original respondents again, but we also sought to recover much of their past lives before the first interview. What we saw was the way in which, over an educational history much longer than most people experience, these mature students were able to, or in some cases were forced to, rework their relationship to the educational world in a way that was incremental rather than planned. They worked upon their own biographies, renegotiating their relationship to the potentially determining forces of class, gender and individual history. They tended to see themselves as individuals, when we might have been tempted to see them merely as members of a social group, and in so doing themselves strengthened the argument of Abrams, that individuals must be seen in terms of their histories as being in a process of 'becoming' rather than in a 'state of being' (Abrams, 1982: 267).

In relation to adult and continuing education, the point has, of course, more than academic significance, since to widen and maintain educational opportunities beyond the conventional ages for the various levels of education, requires a belief in the possibility, to use Hopper and Osborn's phrase, of correcting 'selection errors'. But it requires more than that. Woodley and his colleagues noted how 'intricate' and 'almost unique' was the map of the educational route of each individual in their study (Woodley *et al.*, 1987: 67). Acceptance of this requires a redefinition of the whole process of selection, which has implications, not only at the level of central government policy, but also for the attitudes and practices of individual institutions. To redefine a failure as a success must always imply a criticism of the 'efficiency' of the institution that created the failure in the first place, threatening notions of professional judgement and of educational stan- dards, neither of which can ever be divorced from the primary selective function of education.

Another concern with reproduction theories was the need to find space within them for utility or rationality theories. Hence in the introduction we rehearsed briefly the educational theory of Raymond Boudon and, in particular, his concepts of primary and secondary effects and of social distance (Boudon, 1974). We used these ideas very freely in relating them to gender rather than stratification, but they have been useful in exploring the educational careers of our respondents. This was particularly so in looking at the 'rationality' factor involved in decisions associated with secondary effects, and in sketching the social distance they travelled. Boudon's is a pessimistic theory, created at a time when post-war optimism about the ability of educational opportunity to promote widespread social mobility had faded. It was a pessimism that spread to discussions of gender and education as well as of class and education. The women in our study challenged that pessimism, not in any numerical sense (not even 43 swallows make a summer), but in the sense that they demonstrated a capacity to negotiate the secondary effects of both gender and class and to use educational opportunities to create social and economic opportunities.

No doubt they were special, certainly relatively well educated in their initial schooling and beyond, and, as we have tried to indicate, some seed of motivation or vision had not infrequently been sown in their educational histories that eventually germinated into the ambition to reach higher education. Nevertheless, they illustrate the possibility of engineering social opportunities through education, if only educational routes can be kept open long enough. Educational opportunities are necessary, but not, however, sufficient; what our limited evidence suggests is that for educational opportunities to be sought, there has to be a reconfiguration of the circumstances and outlook of the potential returner. In effect, this means that the world in which the secondary effects operate has to be changed in some way that affects the balance of those costs and benefits that Boudon deems so important in the calculation of educational value (Boudon, 1974: 30). Not surprisingly, amongst our respondents we found that the key to reshaping the vision of the future lay frequently in some aspect of their lives associated with gender; in a reassessment of the life-cycle as children grew up, as a renegotiation of the relationship to the labour market as careers became blocked or became of more significance, and as a process of rebuilding the self as still gendered but differently so. Both sponsorship and necessity were involved in this process of reconfiguration.

In the relatively untheorized area of adult education, the influence of Hopper and Osborn has been considerable, and we have made use of their concepts of relative deprivation and of 'warming up' and 'cooling out'. They are not, however, without their critics. For example, Woodley and his colleagues cast doubt on the general theory of Hopper and Osborn, that adult students in higher education would be likely to have followed 'inconsistent' educational routes (Woodley *et al.*, 1987). Their findings (which include a much broader spectrum of adult students) suggest that many of their respondents left school with the appropriate qualifications for the institution they attended; that is with no qualifications from secondary modern schools and with A levels from grammar schools. They argue that they could find 'large numbers of highly successful school-leavers who were in no way "rejected" by the school system'; equally, of those who left school early, 'the majority either chose to do so or were forced to by home circumstances, rather than being literally "rejected"' (Woodley *et al.*, 1987: 68). This leads Woodley and his colleagues to question the value of the 'systems terminology' used by Hopper and Osborn and particularly the idea that the 'system' labels individuals as rejects. Rather they argue, 'it may well be that what are crucial for the individual's definitions of their abilities and their educational aspirations for the future are not the labels that the system hands out (e.g. "failure" or "success") but the ones they negotiate for themselves' (Woodley *et al.*, 1987: 68).

It should be said, however, as we noted in the introduction, that Hopper and Osborn themselves stress the importance of the subjective notion of relative deprivation in their modification of their original hypothesis, but the point is nevertheless important. Our evidence is not on a scale that would allow us fully to enter this debate, but it would tend to confirm the significance of the modifications that Hopper and Osborn made to their original hypothesis. The 'system', as Woodley and his colleagues suggest, does not simply reject, but it does set evaluative criteria. How individuals relate to those criteria is, of course very much related to their perception of Boudon's secondary effects.

What our 43 case studies illustrate, above all else, is the importance of trying to understand the way in which the individuals articulate their relationship both to structural forces of a more diffuse character (class and gender), and to more formal 'systems' such as education. It may be that one of the problems cultural reproduction theories have is that they see education as too akin to class or gender. The systemic metaphor has at least the virtue of stressing the qualities of formal organization, and of formally legitimated boundaries and distinctions. From the point of view of the individual, the relationship to a system differs from the relationship to structures in that the latter is mediated through cultural rules that (if the hegemonic process is successful) are internalized whilst in the case of the former the relationship will always be more self-consciously and 'rationally' articulated.

One further question raised by the Hopper/Osborn thesis is its historical origin. It was generated in the context of a post-war British educational system which, when children reached the age of 11, separated a minority destined for an academic secondary education from the majority, most of whom, until the 1970s, left school without formal certification. This leads Woodley and his colleagues to suggest that:

> the increasing speed of economic and technological change, leading to a growing need for adult retraining to fit new occupations or to compensate for the collapse of previously dependable ones, makes their view of all adult participation as problematic seem a little dated.
>
> (Woodley *et al.*, 1987: 7)

But they go on to question whether comprehensive secondary education and expanded vocational further education have reduced the number of 'selection errors'. Indeed, they go beyond Hopper and Osborn to suggest that the growth of non-manual as against manual occupations results in a situation where:

> older workers may find it necessary to acquire new qualifications which will put them on an equal footing with their younger successors, or they may see new opportunities for promotion with new qualifications which would not have been apparent previously.

> (ibid.)

We would agree with Woodley and his colleagues that there is no reason to suppose the present educational system any less prone to 'error' than its predecessor. As a selective system it is infinitely more complex, formally, that it was 25 years ago, but this may do no more than increase the scope for feelings of relative deprivation, especially if there really is an increase in the speed of economic and technological change. More immediately relevant from the point of view of this study and less contentious as a generalization is the rapid change in the relationship of women to the labour market. Hopper and Osborn were able to do little more than hint at the way in which a younger generation of women experienced more frustration than their elders in their relationship to education, domesticity and the labour market. The accounts of our respondents give much stronger and detailed evidence of that frustration, but they also indicate the centrality of the education system to its alleviation.

The most tentative of our explorations was into the relationship between an expressive counter-culture, education, gender and the class structure of advanced capitalist societies. Arnot, in her discussions of class and gender, has already identified the possible value of the theoretical work of Bernstein in this area (Arnot, 1982). Particularly interesting is her suggestion that the codes of 'masculinity' and 'femininity' relate to Bernstein's discussion of weak and strong classification and framing. In Bernstein's theory, these clearly have some relationship to the concepts of the 'individual' and the 'person' that we have discussed. Bernstein explored these concepts in relation to class, but it may well be that they have as much if not more relevance to gender. What was abundantly clear from our evidence was that our respondents took the concept of the 'person' with them into higher education, that it was probably supported there by the predominantly arts, education and social science courses they were taking, and that it was only partially modified by re-entry into the labour market. There they were drawn towards jobs (teaching and social work especially) where expressive values could, with some legitimacy, counter instrumental values.

Exploring this further would take us into complex discussions about the problems of describing the class structure of advanced capitalist societies and of the place of women in it, which would take us well beyond the scope of this book. Our evidence is limited to a rather special group of women who reached the academic apex of the educational system and who, as far as we could tell, were mostly entrenched in middle-class professional occupations at the time of the second interview. What our evidence does suggest, however, is the potential value of exploring class, not just as something that can reinforce gender structures, but as something which, within the many factions of the middle classes, can, as Bernstein suggests, find room for colonizing counter-cultures, which are distinctively 'feminine'.

Careers

There is great variety in our respondents' careers, tracing their lifespans to date. If we study pathways between paid and unpaid work, as well as between and within occupations, complexity takes over. But we have argued that – despite reticence about career ambition and a preference for the idea of education as personal development – many respondents saw education as a resource that would enable them to enter public life on better terms and to negotiate more effectively the boundary between public and private life. This last section, then, examines public careers from school leaving to last known occupation, with a view to assessing respondents' uses of education in these terms.

We identified a number of patterns. A small group had used their degrees to further existing careers, or to give them new direction. Belinda was a career nurse with 16 years experience at first interview; she was again in NHS work at second interview, but now in general management. A degree was not an essential prerequisite for her current status, but must have helped in this transition. Jean, too, had used the degree to enhance a librarianship career, moving from assistant work to a professional post. This might be seen as a classic pathway for men in occupations that sponsor employees through degrees (for example, the police), though in these cases no sponsorship was involved.

A second group found it difficult to use their education in careers at all. These included those most eloquent about the personal meaning of education; but working life continued as it might have without their degree. For Isabel, who was already qualified in librarianship, the degree was never seen as a key to open new doors. Others expressed disappointment or frustration, the feeling that better employment might have been expected. Objective and subjective assessment of these situations might not always be the same. Val, in secretarial work, expressed a clear sense that she was better off with her degree than she would have been without it; Dorcas was disappointed by her inability to find a new career, though she was doing work that required her degree qualification. Family commitments and restricted geographical mobility, health, and discrimination on grounds of gender and age, had played a significant part in these situations.

Brown and Webb (1993) emphasize the negative aspects of employment experience for mature women students, contrasting them with younger students and with men, and drawing attention to their poor experience in the private sector. They are undoubtedly right to argue that degrees do not give such women the same opportunities as male and younger students. There is a danger that such arguments end by underplaying the significance of education to women, whose personal comparison is more often between earlier and later life rather than between themselves and comparable men. We would argue that for the majority of our respondents, their subjective and objective experience was of new opportunity, in which education had played a vital part. We therefore end our study on a more positive note, with the two groups whose pathways were of distinctive and new achievement, and with representatives who have articulated their experience more colourfully than we could ourselves.

The third and fourth patterns were more characteristic of our respondents. The third pathway began in one career – nursing or radiography, Civil Service were typical – and ended in another, mainly in teaching, management or social work; it applied to 7 out of the 23. Fourth was the pathway from shop, office or bank to management or professional careers; 9 out of our 23 second interview respondents followed this route. These pathways are distinctively female in a number of respects. Firstly, both origins and destinations are typically female occupations. Secondly, both pathways involve a 'fresh start' (which may be – but not necessarily – associated with a career break for children). Thirdly, this fresh start takes place in one group despite experience of a careered occupation. As in Chapter 7, these last two pathways will be illustrated with case studies, so that we may finish our study with our respondents. Helen represents the first group, beginning from a long established career in nursing, and Susan, with office and housework behind her, the second.

Helen

Having done well at school, Helen began nursing as 'a sort of reaction', wanting to immerse herself in 'something more practical'. She gained 19 years experience as a staff nurse and sister, five or six years of it part-time. She found nursing 'very rewarding':

> That's the most rewarding aspect in nursing – to get contact with all sorts of people . . . not only ill ones, less ill ones, young ones and old ones, which you get anyway, but all the different social strata. You know when I nursed miners, that was totally new.

She 'fitted fairly happily' into the gendered world of health care, and 'for a time naturally moved up and on'. Helen had a more continuous career pattern up to this point than most women of her generation. She had a year as a housewife, but coped with family demands by resisting career opportunities and moving into part-time work:

> So I spent the last five or six years working part time in not such an inspiring job . . . That had a lot to do with it I think . . . had I moved on

into nursing management, where it would have gone otherwise I may never left it . . . I'd run a ward for several years, taught the student nurses, and managed the ward – which is very rewarding – your own thing – some influence. That had replaced an academic career – management – and I think that was taken away from me when I worked part time. I just filled in.

Helen acknowledged other reasons for returning to study. She had a reaction to her earlier reaction 'a great desire to do something more academic'. A degree in Oriental languages obviously met these needs. 'Doing what I've been doing over the last 18 months has made me an obviously happier person.' The experience was one of 'getting acquainted, of getting into things which interest me or are meaningful to me which have been closed to me for some 20 years'. While Helen said yes to questions about the significance of qualifications for getting a job, it was the educational rewards that dominated this first interview. Any planning for a future career was in the background.

Graduation left Helen feeling unprepared. 'I really didn't know what to do. Because Oriental Languages didn't build on anything I had done before.' Helen's school and career success seemed to have left her with more confidence than other respondents, and this was the first indication of such uncertainty. It took two years – 'I did terrible clerical work for less pay than I would have then got in unemployment benefit' – before reaching a translating job at GCHQ. This used the linguistic and writing skills acquired at university. It gave economic security for present and future (she was divorced): 'I did have family commitments, but I had to look for full-time work for financial reasons . . . a reasonable pension had to be a consideration at my age.' And it was enjoyable work that met her intellectual needs in a way that nursing had not.

Helen's emphasis in the first interview was on the intellectual rewards of study, and lack of career planning was evident in the second. But from the relative security of occupational success, she put as strong an emphasis on career as anyone in the interviews:

> I wanted to do it as a basis of a new life, a new career and a new life . . .
> It was a means to an end, and I think it should be. I don't think it should
> be just a hobby, that's somehow wrong. It should give you more, it
> should make much more of a change to you and you should want to use
> it. Part of the change should be that you want to use it. It shouldn't be
> like a course of flower arranging. I feel that it's given me so much and
> that I should give something back, pass it on.

Other people had found Helen's decision to give up nursing for a degree almost inexplicable: 'People didn't think it was a step up; they thought it was a bit of a mad thing to do . . . I might not get the degree or I may harm my career in nursing.' But she achieved exactly what she wanted, and 'I think it's all been related to education'; 'I feel that I'm doing what I really should be doing . . . I got exactly the job I wanted . . . I can be the person I am.'

Susan

Susan passed the 11 plus, but was sent to a secondary modern school, and left after O levels to do clerical work:

> I thought an office would be a respectable kind of a job – that was the ideal – you could go dressed up. So I went into an office. I felt I'd achieved something by *that* really – I was totally ignorant of what the world of work was like but I did think . . . I'd done pretty well – better than a dead-end job.

Reality was otherwise: monotonous work typing standard letters, which she coped with by 'always asking for transfers to different offices to try something different'. She worked to male bosses 'and you were definitely underdogs. Nobody considered you might be capable of getting on – they all expected you to just work in a typing pool till you either got married or left'.

This she did, having four children, and spending 13 years as a housewife. Marriage was not a success; motherhood and housewifery brought rewards for a while, but, 'I thought I'm a person as well. I also like reading books, dancing. I shouldn't be told that you can do that all day and nothing else, so why should I be told that I'd got to be a housewife for the rest of my life?'

She began to think about getting qualifications, preparing for when her youngest daughter started school. Her educational experience left uncertainty about her abilities, and she experimented with A levels. At that point 'I didn't in my wildest dreams think that I could ever get a degree', but needed to 'find out what I *was* made of.' This was followed by an Open University foundation course and a local degree in humanities. At this point in her account of education, careers took second place to questions of personal development. But she did say that she thought 'women are looking for more satisfaction in a career whereas men are looking for more success'.

After graduating, it took Susan two or three years to establish herself. She was rejected for teacher training courses and instead took a Masters degree in information technology. Lack of a maths A level prevented training as a computing teacher, so she took office work with the idea of filling the gap. However, she now realized the possibilities of teaching in further education and offered herself part-time. This led to a temporary post:

> It was a real shortage area . . . people were desperately needed, not so much with a science background, but with an arts background, particularly communication skills, because the main emphasis on using computers these days is not programming, it is running business

applications . . . and that is the area really that I was suited for. It's worked out very well. I'd been there for about five months when a full-time post came up and I applied for that and got it and I've been there ever since. I asked to do my teacher training and the county council actually paid for it, one day a week for two years. So I've done very well, apart from coming out of university and being a bit lost and going a bit astray. I've got a very fulfilling job, and I've five years experience.

Being a woman was an advantage:

There were so many women coming back to retrain, after having children and so many people who were 25 plus, who . . . suddenly realized that they had to get into this huge revolution . . . Women wanted a woman teacher.

Susan's degree took her well beyond anything she had imagined or planned. She saw it as giving confidence and acquiring resources rather than as leading to a particular place: 'it was all geared to establishing myself as employable, I couldn't visualize myself, I hadn't got the confidence to see myself in any high position . . . of authority'. And five years on she still evinced surprise at the consequences:

I can't quite take it in sometimes that I have got a job where I am given a good degree of responsibility and freedom to do it my own way. Authority over people even and that my voice counts . . . I can argue about curriculum design and education policy. I can put forward points of view and people listen, and I find that rather amazing!

Education had costs, especially in terms of relationships with others, but it gave Susan economic security, carrying her through periods as a single parent. She loved her work, but seemed to exemplify her earlier idea of enjoying the 'satisfaction' rather than aiming single-mindedly for 'success'. She also felt comfortable with the balance she was now able to achieve between career and domesticity. 'I'm not totally career-minded either, I want a home life and I like the things at home and I like my own friends and my own activities, so I'm not obsessed with it. I just feel that it does provide you with a nice balance.'

Susan – along with others whose work experience was purely clerical, a prelude to a career as a housewife – had travelled a great distance. In retrospect, she described her need for change and the part that her degree had played:

I was desperately looking for change . . . For 18 years I had been doing everything that people had told me I should do. I was told to get married, to have kids, you should look after your parents. And I got married at 18 and for 18 solid years I did what other people told me to do and I wasn't happy doing it.

A degree alone was not an answer to her problems, 'I had to go on and train afterwards', but it was the crucial – though uncertain – step that made others possible. She has the last word, for herself and many others: 'I'm a person that had that potential, obviously, but it could so easily have been lost.'

Appendix

First interview schedule

1 Last year at school – school
(a) What did school mean to you in the last year or so?
    Was it a place for getting on?
      filling in time?
    Did you like it?
      loathe it?
      feel hostile to it?
(b) Were you interested/involved in it?
      detached from it?
    What about exams? what did they mean to you?
    Were you ever a prefect or monitor?
(c) What were your main preoccupations outside school at this time?
    Was school a place you wanted to escape from?
    Did you ever think of staying longer in education?
      at school?
      in further education?
      in higher education?
    Would more education have seemed to have any point?
(d) What was the educational background of your parents?
      of your brothers?
      of your sisters?

2 Last year at school – thinking about the future
(a) Work
    Did you think in terms of a career?
    Did you think of work as a stopgap before marriage and children?
    Or did you see yourself working a substantial part of your life?
    Did it matter what kind of job it was? clerical? manual?
    What was the occupational background of your parents?
      of your brothers?
      of your sisters?

(b) Marriage
   What did you think about marriage during the last year or so at school?
   Did you assume you would be married within a few years of leaving school?
   What was the attitude of your mother? your father? your school friends?
   Was marriage thought of as an economic necessity for a woman?
      as a romantic 'happy-ever-after'?
(c) Motherhood
   What ideas about motherhood did you hold at that time?
   Did you assume that marriage and motherhood necessarily went together?
   Did you think of motherhood and bringing up children as mother's duty?
      as a major source of fulfilment for a woman?

3 Actual work/family/educational history
Could you help me to fill in the exact details of your work and family history?

4 Interim period
How did experience match up to expectations?
(a) Experience of work
   Did you experience boredom/frustration?
   Did you experience involvement/companionship?
   Do you think the fact that you were a woman affected your experience of work?
      in the way you handled the experience?
      in the way that others treated you?
(b) Marriage
   Has your attitude to marriage changed since you left school?
   Has your experience of marriage changed your attitude?
   Was marriage something for which you feel you were well prepared?
      ill-prepared?
(c) Housewife
   Has the experience of being a housewife been a socially rewarding one?
      an isolating one?
(d) Motherhood
   Has the experience of motherhood/looking after children been satisfying?
      boring?
      frustrating?
      isolating?

5 Deciding to return
(a) Was there any change in family circumstances that made you feel the need for change?
      end of marriage?
      divorce finalized?
      children growing up?
   How decisive were any of these factors? Did they initiate a decision? confirm a decision?
(b) Was there a change in your assessment of the family situation?
      'had not had any children'
      'could not see myself getting married'
      'converted to feminism'

(c) Did you feel you had anything to escape from?
    being a housewife?
    dull, routine job?
    'depressing existence in the home is now unthinkable'
    'there should be more to life than secretarial work or housework'
    'I was terribly depressed working in an office'
(d) Would you say that you drifted into higher education? or that you had to make a more positive effort or struggle?
(e) Did you consider any alternatives to returning to higher education? Why did you reject them?

6 Expectations in returning to higher education
(a) Could you describe yourself as needing education?
    or is it an interesting new hobby?
    something different?
    like an expensive holiday?
(b) What do you expect to gain by returning to education? Can I suggest some things that might be important to you?
    (i)   Qualifications for a job
         better job?
         different job?
         How much are you prepared to put up with in terms of intellectual boredom? frustration? confusion?
    (ii) Education is very important in conferring status on people.
         Was this important to you?
         Being on an equal footing with friends/family
         'After marrying graduate – felt inadequate and lonely'
         Do you expect education to give you more authority in your relationships with other people?
         If not authority, what word would you use?
    (iii) Those who are successful in the educational system sometimes talk about education as something which enriches oneself – leads to self-fulfilment. Is this idea of self-fulfilment important to you?
         What does it mean to you?
            'changed me from a subservient housewife to a thinking human being'
            Does this quotation suggest self-fulfilment or enhanced status?
            Does learning for its own sake carry its own reward?
    (iv) Given the antipathy/envy that many people feel towards 'intellectuals' do you think more education is going to expand or contract the scope of your personal relationships?
(c) What kinds of opposition have you had to face?
    Has guilt about family commitments been important?
(d) What makes it possible to cope with all the difficulties of returning to education at this stage?
    What ideas do you hold on to when things go wrong?
(e) The female preference for arts and social science subjects is still quite strong even among mature students. Have you any views about why this should be so? Are women (even as mature students) looking for something different (from men) from education?

(f) Given that jobs and status are so often decided by educational qualifications, must women be educated to the same extent as men to be treated as equals?
Is it, then, still men who lay down the ground rules?
Are there any alternatives to this?

7 Experience of higher education
Would you say, now you are on a higher-education course, that your expectations were over-romantic?
or have been fully met?

Second interview schedule

Experience and expectations of higher education
When we asked you in the first interview about your expectations of education, we were interested to know how you felt it would affect you in public terms – jobs/careers – and in more personal ones – personal development, relationships with other people.

This interview picks up these two themes, and we now hope to take a longer-term view of your educational experience in these areas:

'A better job . . . I know it's not a popular view, but it's definitely got a large part for me'

'Psychologically it was very important for me'

Some quotations from earlier interviews are on this sheet for you to reflect on.

Career

1 Experience of work since graduating
Could you describe your career since graduating?
Has your experience of work since graduating been of
job/career?
boredom/frustration?
involvement/companionship?
are these different from before?
Since you graduated, has being a woman affected your experience of work?
in the way you handled it?
in the way others treated you?
is this different from before?
Has employment in this period given you economic security?
independence?
how does it compare with previous experience?

2 Impact of higher education on career
A number of our respondents talked of education giving them a new career?

'Problems getting a job without qualifications'

'I wanted a career rather than a job'

'previous work left me no legacy to pick up later on'

'management had been an alternative to an academic career, but that was taken away from me when I went part-time'

Do any of these apply to you?
Has education fulfilled the role you intended in career terms?
Has it taken you beyond your intentions?
Do you feel education has failed you?
  in finding better employment?
  in fitting you for employment?

3 *Other influences on career*
Have you tried to further your career through more courses?
Would you say that new opportunities have come from outside education?
Can you imagine where you might have been without higher education?

Identity

4 *Status*
Some of you were surprised – but not necessarily pleased – by the way being a student affected your status and the way other people thought of you:

'It was a source of amazement to me that people suddenly saw me in a different light'

'I know it confers status – and I'm really sad that it does.'

'Even as a student I have more status than as a wife and mother.'

Do any of these comments apply to you?
Looking back over the period since your degree, have such changes been enduring?

5 *Authority*
There was some ambivalence about the suggestion that education conferred authority.

'In dealing with certain people, it holds a lot of sway which I abuse.'

'That grieves me really, that although you make new friends, you have to lose other people, because I'm still the same person . . . I don't do it to get more authority over other people – I'm doing it for myself.'

Looking back now, would you say that education has given you more authority in your relationships with others?
If not 'authority', what word would you use?
Has it given you more control over your own life?

'I feel more in control of my life than I did then'

6 *Self-fulfilment*
Most of you thought that self-fulfilment was a very significant goal for you, though again there was some anxiety about the consequences of change:

'I suppose it means deep down being happy, but not the sort of frothy happiness that comes and goes.'

'It isn't a hobby, it is me finding myself . . . I'm a totally different person than I was two years ago'.

'It becomes a major ego trip if you feel that you can cope . . . The amazing sense of achievement must be . . . enormous, perhaps the biggest thing in your life.'

'You can't learn for its own sake . . . if you learn, it changes your attitude . . . you're bound to absorb it and adapt it.'

Do any of these comments reflect your experience of higher education at the time?
Have any changes been enduring?
Do you feel any differently about them now?

7 *Change*
A number of you were looking for change:

'The role of being a wife, a mother or a daughter couldn't be all that your life was about. Your life had to be about yourself'

And a number commented on the extent of change brought about by their educational experience:

'I think it permeates everything . . . It's not just something that's collected and stuffed away . . . It permeates everything, the way you live and everything.'

Could you talk about the extent to which you sought change?
    experienced change at the time?
Looking back, do any such changes seem transitory? transforming?

References

Abrams, P. (1982) *Historical Sociology.* Shepton Mallet, Open Books.

Acker, S. (1987) Feminist theory and the study of gender and education, *International Review of Education,* 33(4), 419–35.

Acker, S. and Piper, D.W. (eds) (1984) *Is Higher Education Fair to Women?* Guildford, SRHE and NFER/Nelson.

Anyon, J. (1983) Intersections of gender and class: accommodation and resistance by working-class and affluent females to contradictory sex-role ideologies. In S. Walker and L. Barton (eds) *Gender, Class and Education.* Sussex, The Falmer Press.

Arnot, M. (1982) Male hegemony, social class and women's education, *Journal of Education,* 164, 64–89.

Arnot, M. (1984) A feminist perspective on the relationship between family life and school life, *Journal of Education,* 166, 5–24.

Beechey, V. (1986) Women's employment in contemporary Britain. In V. Beechey and E. Whitelegg (eds) *Women in Britain Today.* Milton Keynes, Open University Press.

Beechey, V. (1987) *Unequal Work.* London, Verso.

Bernstein, B. (1975) *Class, Codes and Control,* Vol 3. London, Routledge and Kegan Paul.

Blackstone, T. (1987) Education and careers for women and girls: the broken chain, *Policy Studies,* 8, 1–17.

Boudon, R. (1973/4) *Education, Opportunity, and Social Inequality.* New York, Wiley.

Boulton, M. G. (1983) *On Being a Mother: A Study of Women with Pre-school Children.* London, Tavistock.

Bourdieu, P. (1977) Cultural reproduction and social reproduction. In J. Karabel and A. H. Halsey (eds) *Power and Ideology in Education.* New York, Oxford University Press.

Bowles, S. and Gintis, H. (1976) *Schooling in Capitalist America.* New York, Basic Books.

Brannen, J. and Moss, P. (1991) *Managing Mothers: Dual Earner Households after Maternity Leave.* London, Unwin Hyman.

Brennan, J. and McGeever, P. (1987) *CNAA Graduates: Their Employment and their Experience after Leaving College.* London, CNAA.

Brown, A. and Webb, J. (1990) The higher education route to the labour market for mature students, *British Journal of Education and Work*, 4(1), 5–21.

Brown, A. and Webb, J. (1993) Career prospects for mature women students: aspirations and achievements. In J. Evetts (ed.) *Women and Career*. London: Longman.

Brown, J. (1989) *Why Don't They Go to Work? Mothers on Benefit*. Social Security Advisory Council Research Report. London, HMSO.

Brown, G. and Harris, T. (1978) *The Social Origins of Depression: A Study of Psychiatric Disorder in Women*. London, Tavistock.

Connell R. W. (1987) *Gender and Power: Society, the Person and Sexual Politics*. Cambridge, Polity Press.

Cox, R. and Pascall, G. (1994) Individualism, narcissism and self-fulfilment in the experience of mature women students, *International Journal of Lifelong Education*, 13, 2.

David, M. (1980) *The State, the Family and Education*. London, Routledge and Kegan Paul.

Davies, L. (1985) Ethnography and status. In R.G. Burgess (ed.) *Field Methods in the Study of Education*. Sussex, Falmer Press.

Deem, R. (1978) *Women and Schooling*. London, Routledge and Kegan Paul.

Deem, R. (ed.) (1980) *Schooling for Women's Work*. London, Routledge and Kegan Paul.

Delamont, S. (1980) *Sex Roles and the School*. London, Methuen.

Department of Education and Science (1987) *Meeting the Challenge*. White paper on higher education, Cmnd 114. London, HMSO.

Evetts, J. (1988) Managing childcare and work responsibilities, *Sociological Review*, 36(3), 501–31.

Evetts, J. (1990) *Women in Primary Teaching: Career Contexts and Strategies*. London, Unwin Hyman.

Faith, K. (1988) *Towards New Horizons for Women in Distance Education: International Perspectives*. London and New York, Routledge.

Felmlee, D. H. (1988) Return to school – women's occupational attainment, *Sociology of Education*, 61, 29–41.

Finch, J. (1983) *Married to the Job: Wives' Incorporation in Men's Work*. London, Unwin Hyman.

Finch, J. (1984) *Education as Social Policy*. London, Longman.

Fulton, O. (ed.) (1989) *Access and Institutional Change*. Milton Keynes, SRHE/Open University Press.

Gavron, H. (1966) *The Captive Wife*. London, Routledge and Kegan Paul.

Gittins, D. (1985) *The Family in Question: Changing Households and Familiar Ideologies*. London, Macmillan.

Glendinning, C. and Millar, J. (eds) (1987/92) *Women and Poverty in Britain*. Brighton, Wheatsheaf Books.

Gouldner, A. (1979) *The Future of Intellectuals and the Rise of the New Class*. London, Macmillan.

Graham, B. (1991) *Messages from Mature Graduates*. A report by the sub-committee on the employment and training of older graduates. Association of Graduate Careers Advisory Service.

Graham, H. (1983) Caring: A labour of love. In J. Finch and D. Groves (eds) *A Labour of Love: Women, Work and Caring*. London, Routledge.

Grant, R. (1987) A career in teaching, *British Educational Research Journal*, 13(3), 227–39.

Grant, R. (1989) Women teachers' career pathways. In S. Acker (ed.) *Teachers, Gender and Careers*. Lewes, Falmer Press.

Griffin, C. (1985) *Typical Girls? Young Women from School to the Job Market*. London, Routledge and Kegan Paul.

Halsey, A. H. *et al.* (1980) *Origins and Destinations*. Oxford, Clarendon.

Hansard Society (1990) *The Report of the Hansard Society Commission on Women at the Top*. London, The Hansard Society for Parliamentary Government.

Hardhill, I. and Green, A. (1991) Women returners: the view from Newcastle upon Tyne, *Employment Gazette*, 99(3), 147–52.

Harris, C. (1983) *The Family and Industrial Society*. London, George Allen and Unwin.

Harrison, M. J. (1990) Access – the problem and potential, *Higher Education Quarterly*, 44(3), 193–213.

Hawthorne, G. (1970) *The Sociology of Fertility*. London, Collier-Macmillan.

Heath, A. (1974) The rational model of man, *Archiv. Europ. Sociol.*, XV, 184–205.

Hilsum, S. and Start, K. B. (1974) *Promotion and Careers in Teaching*. Slough, NFER.

Hopper, E. (1971) *Readings in the Theory of Educational Systems*. London, Hutchinson.

Hopper, E. and Osborn, M. (1975) *Adult Students: Education Selection and Social Control*. London, Frances Pinter.

Horn, P. (1988) The education and employment of working-class girls, 1870–1914, *History of Education*, 17(1), 71–82.

Hughes, M. and Kennedy, M. (eds) (1984) *Breaking the Mould*. London, Routledge and Kegan Paul.

Hutchinson, E. and Hutchinson E. (1986) *Women Returning to Learning*. London, NEC.

Industrial Relations Services (1991) *Pay and Gender in Britain: A Research Report for the Equal Opportunities Commission*. London, IRS.

Jencks, C. *et al.* (1972) *Inequality: A Reassessment of the Effects of Family and Schooling in America*. New York, Basic Books.

Johnson, R. and Bailey, R. (1984) *Mature Students: Perception and Experiences of Full-time and Part-time Higher Education*. PAVIC Publications.

Joshi, H. (1987). The cost of caring. In C. Glendinning and J. Millar (eds) *Women and Poverty in Britain*. Brighton, Wheatsheaf Books.

Joshi, H. (1991) Sex and motherhood as handicaps in the labour market. In M. Maclean and D. Groves (eds) *Women's Issues in Social Policy*. London and New York, Routledge.

Kamm, J. (1965) *Hope Deferred: Girls' Education in English History*. London, Methuen.

Karabel, J. and Halsey, A. H. (eds) (1977) *Power and Ideology in Education*. Oxford, Oxford University Press.

Lindblom, C. E. (1959) The science of muddling through, *Public Administration Review*, 19, 79–88.

Lindblom, C. E. (1979) Still muddling, not yet through, *Public Administration Review*, 39, 517–32.

Lyons, G. (1981) *Teacher Careers and Career Perceptions*. Windsor, NFER/ Nelson.

MacDonald, M. (1980) Socio-cultural reproduction and women's education. In R. Deem (ed.) *Women and Schooling*. London, Routledge and Kegan Paul.

McLaren, A. T. (1981) Women in adult education: the neglected majority, *International Journal of Women's Studies*, 4(3), 245–57.

McLaren, A. T. (1985) *Ambitions and Realizations: Women in Adult Education*. London, Peter Owen.

McRobbie, A. (1978) Working-class girls and the culture of femininity. In Centre for Contemporary Cultural Studies Women's Group (eds) *Women Take Issue*. London, Hutchison.

Martin, B. (1981) *A Sociology of Contemporary Cultural Change*. Oxford, Blackwell.

Martin, J. and Roberts, C. (1984) *Women and Employment*. London, HMSO.

Morgan, V. (1981) *Late But In Earnest: A Case Study of Mature Women Students at University*. Collected Original Research in Education (CORE), 5, 2, from 9 on 6 to E3 on 7.

Morris, A. E. and Nott, S. M. (1991) *Working Women and the Law: Equality and Discrimination in Theory and Practice*. London, Routledge/Sweet and Maxwell.

Oakley, A. (1974) *Housewife*. Hardmondsworth, Allen Lane.

Oakley, A. (1981) *Subject Women*. Oxford, Martin Robertson.

OPCS (1991) *General Household Survey 1989*. London, HMSO.

Pascall, G. (1986) *Social Policy: A Feminist Analysis*. London, Tavistock.

Pascall, G. (1993) Women in professional careers: social policy developments. In J. Evetts (ed.) *Women and Career*. London, Longman.

Pascall, G. and Cox, R. (1993) Education and domesticity, *Gender and Education*, 5(1), 17–36.

Rees, T. (1992) *Women and the Labour Market*. London, Routledge and Kegan Paul.

Riley, D. (1983) *War in the Nursery: Theories of the Child and Mother*. London, Virago.

Slowey, M. (1987) Adults in higher education: the situation in the United Kingdom. In H. G. Schutze *et al.*, *Adults in Higher Education: Policies and Practice in Great Britain and North America*. Stockholm, Almqvist and Wiksell International.

Slowey, M. (1988) Adult students – the new mission for higher education? *Higher Education Quarterly*, 42(4), 301–16.

Smithers, A. and Griffin, A. (1986) *The Progress of Mature Students*. Manchester, Joint Matriculation Board.

Tarsh, J. (1989) New graduate destinations by age on graduation, *Employment Gazette*, November, 97(1), 581–98.

Titmuss, R. (1958) *Essays on the Welfare State*. London, George Allen and Unwin.

Thompson, J. (1983) *Learning Liberation: Women's Response to Men's Education*. London and Canberra, Croom Helm.

Valli, L. (1986) *Becoming Clerical Workers*. Boston, London and Henley, Routledge and Kegan Paul.

Wagner, L. (1989) National policy and institutional development. In O. Fulton (ed.) *Access and Institutional Change*. Milton Keynes, SRHE/Open University Press.

Walby, S. (1986) *Patriarchy at Work*. Cambridge, Polity Press/Basil Blackwell.

Weil, S. W. (1989) Access: towards education or miseducation? Adults imagine the future. In O. Fulton (ed.) *Access and Institutional Change*. SRHE/Open University Press.

Weiler, K. (1988) *Women Teaching for Change: Gender, Class and Power*. Massachusetts, Bergin and Garvey Publishers.

Willis, P. (1977) *Learning to Labour*. Westmead, Saxon House.

Wolfenstein, M. (1955) Fun morality: an analysis of recent American child-training literature. In M. Mead and M. Wolfenstein (eds) *Childhood in Contemporary Culture*. Chicago, University of Chicago Press.

Wolpe, A-M. (1988) *Within School Walls: The Role of Discipline, Sexuality and the Curriculum*. London, Routledge and Kegan Paul.

Woodley, A. (1984) The older the better? A study of mature student performance in British universities, *Research in Education*, 32, 32–50.

Woodley, A. (1985) Taking account of mature students. In D. Jacques and J. Richardson (eds) *The Future of Higher Education*. Guildford: SRHE and NFER/Nelson.

Woodley, A. *et al.* (1987) *Choosing to Learn: Adults in Education*. Milton Keynes, Open University Press.

Index

The Society for Research into Higher Education

The Society for Research into Higher Education exists to stimulate and co-ordinate research into all aspects of higher education. It aims to improve the quality of higher education through the encouragement of debate and publication on issues of policy, on the organization and management of higher education institutions, and on the curriculum and teaching methods.

The Society's income is derived from subscriptions, sales of its books and journals, conference fees and grants. It receives no subsidies, and is wholly independent. Its individual members include teachers, researchers, managers and students. Its corporate members are institutions of higher education, research institutes, professional, industrial and governmental bodies. Members are not only from the UK, but from elsewhere in Europe, from America, Canada and Australasia, and it regards its international work as amongst its most important activities.

Under the imprint *SRHE & Open University Press*, the Society is a specialist publisher of research, having some 45 titles in print. The Editorial Board of the Society's Imprint seeks authoritative research or study in the above fields. It offers competitive royalties, a highly recognizable format in both hardback and paperback and the world-wide reputation of the Open University Press.

The Society also publishes *Studies in Higher Education* (three times a year), which is mainly concerned with academic issues, *Higher Education Quarterly* (formerly *Universities Quarterly*), mainly concerned with policy issues, *Research into Higher Education Abstracts* (three times a year), and *SRHE News* (four times a year).

The Society holds a major annual conference in December, jointly with an institution of higher education. In 1991, the topic was 'Research and Higher Education in Europe', with the University of Leicester. In 1992, it was 'Learning to Effect' with Nottingham Trent University and in 1993, 'Governments and the Higher Education Curriculum: Evolving Partnerships' at the University of Sussex in Brighton. Future conferences include in 1994, 'The Student Experience' at the University of York.

The Society's committees, study groups and branches are run by the members. The groups at present include:

Teacher Education Study Group
Continuing Education Group
Staff Development Group
Excellence in Teaching and Learning

Benefits to members

Individual

Individual members receive:

- *SRHE News*, the Society's publications list, conference details and other material included in mailings.
- Greatly reduced rates for *Studies in Higher Education* and *Higher Education Quarterly*.
- A 35% discount on all Open University Press & SRHE publications.
- Free copies of the Precedings – commissioned papers on the theme of the Annual Conference.
- Free copies of *Research into Higher Education Abstracts*.
- Reduced rates for conferences.
- Extensive contacts and scope for facilitating initiatives.
- Reduced reciprocal memberships.

Corporate

Corporate members receive:

- All benefits of individual members, plus
- Free copies of *Studies in Higher Education*.
- Unlimited copies of the Society's publications at reduced rates.
- Special rates for its members e.g. to the Annual Conference.

Membership details: SRHE, 344–354 Gray's Inn Road, London, WC1X 8BP, UK. Tel: 071 837 7880
Catalogue: SRHE & Open University Press, Celtic Court, 22 Ballmoor, Buckingham MK18 1XW. Tel: (0280) 823388

GENDER AND SUBJECT IN HIGHER EDUCATION

Kim Thomas

Despite the growing number of studies of gender in education, the topic of gender in higher education has often been ignored. This far-ranging book attempts to redress the balance by an exploration of a number of related issues: why women and men tend to specialize in different subject areas; the experience of being a woman in a 'man's' subject and a man in a 'woman's' subject; whether higher education plays a part in reproducing gender inequality. In particular, the author focuses on the arts/science divide; taking two representative subjects, physics and English, she looks at the way each is constructed by lecturers and students, and the relationship between these constructions and the social construction of gender. She argues that students choose which subject to study on the basis of certain qualities these subjects are seen to hold, and that these qualities have close connections with beliefs about 'masculinity' and 'femininity'. Most students develop a subject loyalty, reinforced by studying the discipline in higher education, but this subject loyalty can be challenged or reinforced by a student's sense of gender identity. The author argues that the boundaries between different disciplines are often artificial and limiting, and for this reason she also looks at attempts in polytechnics to remove interdisciplinary barriers, asking whether subjects such as communications and physical science provide a challenge to traditional university subjects like English and Physics. The author concludes that universities have, on the whole, been complacent about the issue of gender inequality and suggests that a fresh look at current practices is overdue.

This book will be a thought-provoking read for anybody who teaches in higher education, as well as for those specializing in the areas of gender and education and women's studies.

Contents

The question of gender – Feminism and education – The two cultures – Constructing Science – Constructing humanities – Gender identity and science students – Gender identity and humanities students – Conclusion – References – Index.

208pp   0 335 09271 3 (Paperback)   0 335 09272 1 (Hardback)

WOMEN'S EDUCATION

Maggie Coats

This book is about women's education; it is not about education for women. 'Women's education' is education which is possessed or owned by women; education which is provided by women for women, which focuses on the needs of women, and which is designed for and about women.

Maggie Coats celebrates the achievements of women's education over the past twenty years, paying tribute to the women who have been involved in it. She describes and analyses the meaning, development and distinctive characteristics of women's education, arguing that we should build upon the lessons learnt during the last two decades; that we should expand rather than contract provision; and that we should make a long-term commitment to women's education.

Contents

What is women's education? – The background to women's education today – Feminist ideologies and women's education – The case for women-only provision – The curriculum of women-only provision: six case studies – The curriculum of women-only provision: the main themes – The curriculum of women-only provision: recommendations and guidelines – Education or training? The significance of women-only provision – Women's education: challenging the backlash – Appendix – Bibliography – Index.

c176pp   0 335 15734 3 (Paperback)   0 335 15735 1 (Hardback)

THE LEARNING UNIVERSITY
TOWARDS A NEW PARADIGM?

Chris Duke

Chris Duke addresses issues central to the evolution and future of higher
education. He examines assumptions by and about universities, their changing
environments, the new terminologies and their adaptation to new circumstances.
He explores how far universities *are* learning, changing and adapting; and whether
they are becoming different kinds of institutions or whether only the rhetoric is
altering. He is particularly concerned with how far universities, as key teaching and
learning organizations, are adopting the new paradigm of lifelong learning. He
discusses how far the concepts and requirements for institution-wide continuing
education have been identified and internalized in institutional planning; are they,
for instance, reflected in programmes of staff development (in the continuing
education of staff in higher education)? *Is* a new paradigm of university education
and organization really emerging?

Contents
Old assumptions and new practices – Change and higher education: the new discourse –
Mission, aims and objectives – What may be new? – Out of the box: continuing education
university-wide – Finishing school or service station: what mix? – Access, quality and success:
old and new criteria – Staff development and organizational learning – The fallacy of the
ivory tower – Appendix – Bibliography – Index.

160pp   0 335 15653 3 (Paperback)   0 335 15654 1 (Hardback)